The Problem of Asia

The
Problem of Asia
and
Its Effect upon International Policies

BY

A. T. MAHAN, D.C.L., LL.D.
Captain United States Navy

KENNIKAT PRESS
Port Washington, N. Y./London

THE PROBLEM OF ASIA

First published in 1900
Reissued in 1970 by Kennikat Press
Library of Congress Catalog Card No: 70-115204
ISBN 0-8046-1097-5

Manufactured by Taylor Publishing Company   Dallas, Texas

PREFACE

THE onward movement of the world is largely determined, both in rate and in direction, by geographical and physical conditions. Add to them racial characteristics, and we probably have the chief constituents of the raw material, which, under varying impulses from within and without, is gradually worked up into history.

The process of the manufacture is seen in the course of events; but these, whether in current history or in the wholly past, embrace a great mass of details, which, by the various and conflicting directions of their action, not only perplex the inquirer with a sense of utter confusion, but also cover, and to a first glance effectually conceal, the determinative conditions. Such conditions, however, there always are; and these shape and govern the whole range of incidents, often in themselves apparently chaotic in combination, and devoid of guidance by any adequate controlling forces.

In history entirely past, where an issue has been reached sufficiently definite to show that one period has ended and another begun, it is possible for a careful observer to detect, and with some precision to formulate, the leading causes, and to trace the interaction which has produced the result. It is obviously much less easy to discover the character and to fix the inter-relation of the elements acting in the present; still more to indicate the direction of their individual movement, from which conjecture may form some conception as to what shall issue as the resultant of forces. There is here all the difference between history and prophecy.

Nevertheless, although the one study is more certain, the other is more urgent. Past history contains indeed lessons which, well digested, are most valuable for future guidance; but, when the attempt is made to utilize their teachings, contemporary conditions are found to differ so much from those preceding them that application becomes a matter of no slight difficulty, requiring judgment and conjecture rather than imparting certainty. Positiveness in such matters, indeed, is the doubtful privilege of the *doctrinaire*, and commonly unfortunate in the result. The instruction derived from the past must be supplemented by a particularized study of the indications of the future.

Although assuredness of conclusion is denied to this process, we can still be confident that under all surface conditions, present as past, there must lie permanent facts, and factors, the detection and specification of which ascertains at least the existence and character of certain determinative features, and the relations subsisting between them. Even so much is gain; and gain it will remain for the guidance of nations and of mankind, even though it be not possible to forecast the precise combination into which, through the operation of unforeseen events, these various factors will ultimately fall.

The determination of these distinct factors, in a present question of great moment, and, so far as may be, the investigation of their mutual relations, are the objects of the present study. The first paper — The Problem of Asia — aims at the selection and exposition of the great permanent features. It was nearly completed, in its three chapters, by the first of the current year — 1900; and therefore antedates entirely the recent outbreaks in China, although the causes of these were doubtless operative some time before. The second paper, — Effect of Asiatic Conditions upon World Policies, — written in August, attempts to trace the influences that will be exerted by the permanent features, previously noted, upon the passing political conditions, under which present policies have to take shape.

The insertion of the third paper — Merits of the Transvaal Dispute — has been an afterthought. Having had occasion in the other articles to re-affirm more than once my conviction of the essential righteousness of the British cause in South Africa, it has seemed to me pertinent to add thereto, in justification of this belief, a summary of the facts and arguments by which it was reached.

It remains to express my thanks to the proprietors of "Harper's New Monthly Magazine" and of the "North American Review," for their kind permission to reproduce the articles in book form.

A. T. MAHAN.

September, 1900.

CONTENTS

I. THE PROBLEM OF ASIA
From Harper's New Monthly Magazine

CHAPTER I. — MARCH, 1900

	PAGE
The paradox of long and short views	1
Applicable to both personal and corporate life	1
Specially illustrated in world movements	2
World conditions in constant flux	3
Consequent effect upon actions of governments	3
The Present the guardian of the Future	3
Impulse in United States towards expansion	4
Closely related to like movements in Europe	4
Illustrations	4
Effects upon international relations	5
Long and short view illustrated in recent American history	5
Development of the idea of expansion	6
Stopped short once at Hawaii	7
To that point the idea essentially defensive	7
Sudden precipitation of Philippine question	8
Time needed to settle firmly new conditions of national responsibility	9
Necessary nevertheless to consider at once the future to which they point	9
Such consideration facilitates decision in sudden emergencies	10

xii   *Contents*

CHAPTER I. — MARCH, 1900 — *continued*   PAGE
Presence of mind dependent upon preparation . . . 10
Our war with Spain not a disconnected incident . . . 11
Rapid change in attitude of Japan towards United States
    concerning Hawaii 11
Scope of Monroe Doctrine defined 13
Illustrates a general maxim of statesmanship 14
Is not applicable to Asia 15
Force of tradition upon popular conception of Monroe
    Doctrine 16
Principle permanent, application variable 16
Increased importance of European conditions to Amer-
    ican interests 17
Consequent necessity of appreciating European inter-
    national politics 17
The interest of the world centring upon Asia 18
Conditions and circumstances of the question should be
    studied 18
Primary importance of geographical features 18
Political problems closely analogous to military . . . 19
Importance of " communications " to both 19
Facility of transmission the attribute of sea power . . 20
Geographical analysis of Asian Continent 20
Climatic conditions. Monsoons 20
Important middle belt, between 30° and 40° North . . 21
Unstable political conditions in this belt 22
In Asia, division is east and west, movement north and
    south 22
Necessary to study characteristics of movement . . . 22
In political study, impossible to dissociate Eastern Asia
    from Western 23
Present distribution of stable political forces 24
Continuous mass of Russian territory 24

Chapter I. — March, 1900 — *continued*

	Page
Military advantages of Russian position	25
Its points of military weakness	26
The geographical position of Great Britain in Asia	27
Characteristics of British military strength	27
Relation of India to military power of British Empire	27
Intrinsic advantages of India as a base in Asia	28
Effect of British and Russian tenures in Asia upon the policy of the two empires	29
Self-preservation the first natural law of states	29
Scope to grow essential to self-preservation	30
Growth, like evolution, gives rise to conflict	30
Nations are trustees for posterity	30
Recourse to arbitration conditioned by trusteeship	31
The need and right to grow, factors in the Problem of Asia	31
Growth depends on vigor of organization and freedom of intercourse	31
Internal organization a national, not an international question	32
Interchange necessarily involves other peoples	32
Freedom of interchange in Asia, an interest common to all commercial states	33
Consequent jealousy of inimical military influences	33
Movements of acquisition already begun	34
Commercial possibilities of Asia great, but still indefinite	35
The question one of scale rather than proportion	35
Bearing of external communications upon the problem	36
Communications twofold: by sea and by land	36
Suggests the multiform struggle between land and sea power	37
Sea and land power exemplified in Great Britain and Russia	37

Chapter I. — March, 1900 — *continued*

	Page
Superior copiousness and cheapness of water communications	38
Their consequent preponderance in development of Asia	38
Control of communications a question of naval power	38
Mutual influence of land and sea power, when in contact	39
Importance of the Yang-tse-kiang to sea power	41
Interest of commerce in the maintenance of peace	42
Military force essential to secure peace	42
Incapacity of navies to threaten liberty	42
Dependence of Russia upon land communications	42
This condition not susceptible of much modification	43
Consequent disadvantage of Russia for the pursuits of commerce	43
Resultant inevitable tendency to acquire maritime positions	44
Effect upon the policy of other states	45
Obligations of other states to their own people and to the peoples of Asia	45
Complexity and imminence of the Problem of Asia	46

Chapter II. — April, 1900

Russia's predominant land power in Asia	47
Counterbalance by indirect pressure	47
Military meaning of "diversion"	48
Relative mutual effect of flanks and centre of a line	48
Advantages of pressure, or of attack, on a flank	48
Factors essential to durable peace in Asia	49
International uneasiness concerning Asia	49
Danger of failure to weigh conditions, and forecast future	49
Peace within Europe, how preserved at present	50
Analogy in Asia	50
Indirect pressure by control of sea and of commerce	51

CHAPTER II. — APRIL, 1900 — *continued* PAGE

Political danger of granting immunity to so-called "private property" at sea 52
Goods in commercial transit are not "private" property 53
Russia's advance in Asia is by the flanks 55
Its objects, threefold access to the sea 56
Interests and opportunities of other states 57
Objectives of policy in Asia 58
Turkey in Asia and Persia — topographic features . . 58
Present internal and political conditions 58
Advance from such conditions in the past, how effected . 60
Instances — India and Egypt 61
Application to future of Western Asia and of China . . 61
Twofold characteristics of movements now in progress . 62
    1. Upon both flanks.
    2. Antagonism of sea power and land power.
Artificial relation of France to Russia 63
Solidarity of interest in sea powers 63
Particular conditions of each sea power 63
Relative military situations on either flank 64
Importance of Yang-tse to sea power 65
Military situations condition policy 65
Influence of position of Chinese capital 66
Political and military conditions in Western Asia and the Levant 67
Conflicting interests of France and Italy in the Mediterranean 67
French ambitions in the Mediterranean 67
Effects upon security of Suez route 67
Indirect interest of the United States and Japan . . . 68
Military dangers of the Suez route 69
Its decisive military superiority to that by Cape of Good Hope 70

CHAPTER II. — APRIL, 1900 — *continued*

	PAGE
Egypt and Asiatic Turkey by position control Suez route	70
Consequent necessity and effect of political development	70
Development there can begin only from without	72
Its character will depend upon that of the external influence	73
No analogue to the Yang-tse in Levantine Turkey	75
Political effect of railroad from Mediterranean to Persian Gulf	76
Importance of harmony among sea powers	76
Relative commercial value to the world of Eastern and Western Asia	77
Superior military consequence of Western Asia	77
French preponderance in Western Mediterranean	78
Conditions change east of Sicily	78
Present difficulties of sea powers maintaining naval force in the Levant	78
To be met only by establishing local political influence	79
Inalienable strategic importance of Egypt	79
Its central position, and double line of communications	80
Twofold obligation of Great Britain to hold it	80
1. Duty to continue work of regeneration.	
2. Essential to integrity of British Empire.	
Inexpediency of abandoning Suez route	81
Napoleon's saying — "War cannot be made without running risks"	82
True solution of military dilemmas of Suez route	82
Historical importance of Eastern Mediterranean	82
The world's progress east and west, not north and south	83
Significance of Isthmuses of Suez and Panama	84
Situation at Suez more critical than at Panama	84
Effect of these considerations upon political traditions	85

Chapter II. — April, 1900 — *continued*

	Page
Diminished importance of South Africa, and of America south of valley of the Amazon	86
Modifying effect upon Monroe Doctrine	86
Necessity of concentrating national effort by excluding minor issues	86
The future of Asiatic peoples	86
Their general stolid conservatism	87
Effect of external influences	87
Grave possibilities of the Chinese masses	88
Consequent importance of the direction imparted by external impulse	88
Necessity for serious study and prevision	89
The result, the introduction of Eastern peoples into the European commonwealth	90
Racial characteristics must remain	91
Parallel in the assimilation of Roman civilization by Teutonic races	91
The Roman law and the imperial idea	91
Inherited by the centralized Christian Church	91
The Christian tradition the unifying thread of European civilization	92
The grounds for hope	93
Superior political vitality of a community of states over a consolidated empire	94

Chapter III. — May, 1900

Present imminent condition of Asiatic problem	96
Rivalries of external nations	97
Consideration due to native populations	97
Not necessarily due to existing native governments	98
Present uneasiness result of inefficient government	99

Chapter III. — May, 1900 — *continued*

	Page
Necessity for action laid upon foreign states	99
Alternative methods of action	99
Conditions of an efficacious solution	100
1. Political equilibrium among external powers.	
2. Material and spiritual progress of native inhabitants.	
Results to be expected	101
Results attained in Japan	101
Difference in conditions between Japan and China	102
Best development through diversified influences by differing race-types	102
Advantage of strong oppositions in international polity	103
Equilibrium represented by land and sea power in opposing scales	104
Special interest of Teutonic powers	104
Necessity of co-operation	104
Special difficulties attendant upon co-operation of states	104
Need to convince citizens of free states	104
Simplicity of Russian political organization	104
French alliance with Russia	105
Resultant divergence of interests among Latin states	105
France imperfectly Latin in type	105
Consequent defective influence of Latin states in Asiatic problem	106
Slavonic and Teutonic the chief European influences	106
Peculiar relation of Japan to the Asiatic problem	106
Japan essentially a sea power	106
Limitations upon the scope of her action	106
1. Because of limited area and wealth.	
2. Because of restrictedly local character of her interests.	
Similarity of interests in Japan and the Teutonic states	107

CHAPTER III. — MAY, 1900 — *continued*   PAGE

Essential differences of European civilization, as now
    found in both 108
Japan racially Asiatic, adoptively European 108
Advantage of this factor to the Asiatic future . . . 109
Misunderstandings natural between differing race-types 110
How best to be obviated 111
Unanimity the aim, rather than uniformity 111
Necessity of mutual respect between races 111
The Problem of Asia to be approached in this spirit . 113
Conservative inertia of Asiatic peoples 114
Japan the sole exception 114
Antagonism of type in Slav and Teuton 114
Conflict between their interests 115
Opposition must be recognized in order to conciliation . 115
Land power the prerogative of Slavs 116
Sea power that of the Teuton states 116
These conditions, being essential, cannot be reversed . 116
They may, however, be modified 116
Racial and national interests demand such modification . 117
Russia's need of freer access to the sea 117
Opposing exigencies of the Teuton situation 117
Direction in which the claim of Russia should be cor-
    dially conceded 120
Essential necessity of Yang-tse valley to the sea powers 120
Their secure access to it to be cordially conceded . . 120
Co-operation between naval states imperative 121
Land power more menacing to China than sea power . 121
Reasons 121
Commerce essentially tends to peace 122
The future of Asia dependent upon military considera-
    tions 124
The question of communications 125

Chapter III. — May, 1900 — continued

	Page
Communications dominate war	125
The sea the chief medium of world communications	125
Consequent influence of sea power upon Asian problem	126
Sea power exerts its effect by indirect pressure, — by diversion	126
Right to control maritime commerce is therefore essential to it, and not to be surrendered	126
The three Teutonic states — Germany, Great Britain, and the United States	127
Only Germany and Great Britain directly interested in Levant	127
Requirements to the establishing of their position there	127
Peculiar interest of Great Britain	128
Interest of the United States, indirect but real	129
Indifference of American citizens to external questions	130
Urgent necessity to amend this defect	131
Pacific Ocean and Eastern Asia the coming chief centre of world interest	131
Interests there of the Teutonic states not the same, yet similar	133
Conditions of efficient mutual support	134

    1. Participation in a common purpose, rather than assumption of a literal obligation.
    2. Candid recognition of respective interests and spheres of responsibility.
    3. Abstention from permanent formal obligations.
    4. Retention of independence in individual state action.
    5. Results: co-operation, not alliance.

Modifying effect of new conditions upon applications of Monroe Doctrine	135

Chapter III. — May, 1900 — *continued*   Page
 Only the United States directly interested in the Caribbean and its Isthmus 136
 Increasing mutual comprehension between the English-speaking communities 139
 Promises endurance, because resulting from permanent conditions 139
 Evidenced in our war with Spain and in the Transvaal hostilities 140
 Tendency of mankind to aggregate into groups greater than existing nationalities 141
 War a principal instrument in this process, historically. Instances 141
 Justification of war between United States and Spain, and of Great Britain in South Africa 142
 Security of the foundations for Anglo-American co-operation 144
 Ethnic relation of Germany to the English-speaking communities 144
 Relation of Italy to present world movements . . . 145

II. EFFECT OF ASIATIC CONDITIONS UPON WORLD POLICIES

From North American Review, November, 1900

 Extraordinary events since the writing of preceding papers 147
 Common effect upon European nations 147
 The United States and Japan members of European commonwealth 147
 Japan's claims to be so considered 148
 Parallel in Teutonic entrance into Roman civilization . 149

II. ASIATIC CONDITIONS — *continued*

                                                                         PAGE

Difference between the conditions of the Roman world then, and Christian civilization now 149

Japan the only Asiatic participant of European progress 150

Influence of insular environment 151

Recent events have not changed permanent conditions . 152

They do not indicate any change of Asiatic characteristics 152

Consequently, no permanent change in national policies 153

Momentary necessity for combined action of European states 153

Obligation of states during such a passing moment . . 153

Permanent policy resumes sway afterwards 154

Europe's community, as well as divergence, of interest in Asia 154

Recent declaration of policy by United States Government 155

Consistent with our past line of action 155

Course of governments controlled by public opinion . 156

Necessity for individual citizens to study the conditions 156

Imperfect knowledge the source of popular fickleness . 157

Summary of world conditions 157

General competition for world's commerce 158

Effort to compass end by appropriation of territory, or by establishment of influence 159

Results in international antagonism, resting upon armed force 159

Fixity of political tenure in Europe and America . . 159

Analogous condition in Africa and the islands of the sea 159

Different political status of Asia 160

Necessary policy of the maritime powers 161

Particular conditions of the United States 162

	PAGE
II. ASIATIC CONDITIONS — *continued*	
Commercial and political importance of the Yang-tse valley	164
Present close contact of Eastern and Western civilizations	165
Interaction can no longer be avoided	166
Guidance all that can be attempted	166
Freedom of thought and speech requisite, as well as freedom to trade	166
Principal objects in dealing with Chinese question	167
1. Prevention of preponderant control by any one state.	
2. Insistence upon the "open door" for speech, as well as for commerce.	
Baselessness of outcry against missionary effort	168
Christianity an effective part of Western civilization	168
Critical importance of present moment	169
Necessity for United States to prepare for her part in the future	169
Preparation of purpose and preparation of power	169
Preparation of power implies also curtailment of needless efforts	170
Policy of the United States clearly defined by its government	170
Diverse in spirit from that of some other states	171
The difference calls for watchfulness	171
The "open door" can be maintained only by readiness to enforce it	172
National influence depends upon evidence of purpose and of power	172
Matters cannot safely be allowed to drift	173
Incapacity of China to develop unaided	174
Aim of recent reactionary movement	174

II. Asiatic Conditions — *continued*

	PAGE
Must be resisted; by force, if necessary	174
This will be done, even if the United States stands aside	174
The signs of the times	175
The Yang-tse valley the great field for commerce and for sea power	176
Powers in competition upon the field	177
Power of independent action always limited	177
Consequent necessity for co-operation	178
Co-operation rests upon community of interests and standards	178
Does not renounce individual responsibility	178
Implies also division of labor	179
Co-operation not only local in Asia	179
Distributed likewise between the ocean lines of communication	179
Two chief lines — from Europe and from America	179
Europe *via* Suez, America *via* Panama	179
Decisive points on each line	180
Under co-operation, the American line is the *charge* of the United States, as well as her interest	180
Our claim to preponderant consideration in the Caribbean practically conceded	180
Not a barren triumph only, but a responsibility	181
United States needs effective naval force in both Pacific and Atlantic	181
Communications by canal liable to interruption	182
Military advantages of the "interior line"	182
Military use of canal depends mainly on the solidity of our naval power in the Caribbean	183
Risk cannot be wholly eliminated from warfare	183
Probable security, however, obtainable	184
First element of security an adequate fleet	184

II. ASIATIC CONDITIONS — *continued*   PAGE
    Conditions of adequacy defined 184
    Great Britain formerly opposed to our preponderance in
        the Caribbean 185
    Reasons for her change of attitude in this respect . . 185
    Her interest now that we be in naval predominance there 186
    Probability of her moral support 186
    Her attitude during the recent war with Spain . . . 187
    Significance of moral support, when based upon com-
        munity of interests 187
    Requires, however, evidence of due preparation of pur-
        pose and of power 189
    Bitterness towards Great Britain shown by some Amer-
        ican citizens 189
    Exaggerated inferences as to action thence drawn . . 190
    Sentiments, bitter or otherwise, permanent only when
        based on actual interest 190
    The United States and Great Britain have common actual
        interests and common standards 190
    Bitterness therefore transient, not reflecting real interests 190
    The appreciation of such factors by statesmen . . . 190
    Contrary effect upon them of backwardness in military
        and naval preparation 191
    Discussion of general conditions governing naval force
        needed by United States 191
    Difference of level between Eastern and Western civili-
        zations 191
    Consequent danger when barriers disappear 192
    Importance of the Anglo-Saxon type to the final result 192
    Continuous vitality and power shown by it since known
        to history 192
    Duty of the United States to contribute to future racial
        action 193

II. ASIATIC CONDITIONS — *continued*   PAGE
 Prejudices to be sacrificed to this end 194
 The Pacific and the East, the sphere for our external exertion 194
 Bearing of Great Britain's friendship upon the size of our navy 195
 Dependence of Great Britain upon her navy vital . . 197
 The United States self-dependent for the necessaries of existence 198
 Considerations determining the size of the United States navy 198
 Superior importance of providing an adequate number of trained seamen 199
 This element of force generally overlooked 199
 Retrenchment of external responsibilities by United States 201
 Application of Monroe Doctrine extended too far . . 201
 The valley of the Amazon suggests a possible broad dividing belt 202

III. MERITS OF THE TRANSVAAL DISPUTE
From the North American Review, March, 1900

 Merits of the Transvaal dispute 203

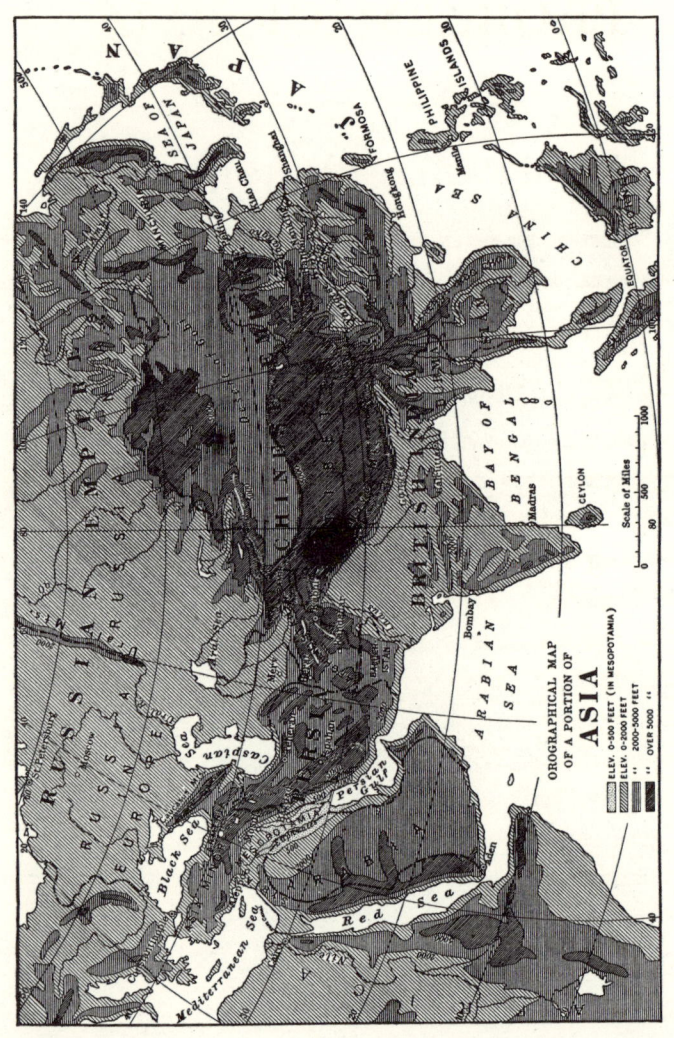

THE
PROBLEM OF ASIA

CHAPTER I

IN order to efficiency of action, whether in personal or in corporate life, we have to recognize the coincident necessities of taking long views and of confining ourselves to short ones. The two ideas, although in contradiction logically, are in practice and in effect complementary, as are the centripetal and centrifugal forces of the universe; unless both are present, something is wanting to the due balance of judgment and of decision. This is, indeed, but one of many illustrations that the philosophy of life is best expressed in paradox. It is by frank acceptance of contrary truths, embracing both without effort to blend them, that we can best direct our course, as individuals or as nations, to successful issues. This observation receives practical illustration in the admitted political maxim that a strong opposition is essential to successful representative government. Thus it is again that only by a minute mastery of details can a solid foundation be laid upon which to build opinion; yet unless details are thrust aside, and reflection fastens upon the leading features only of a problem of conduct, it is difficult, if not impossible, clearly to perceive the mutual relations of the parts and their proportions to the whole, upon a just sense of which depends correctness of appreciation, with consequent discretion of action.

Beyond all other movement, beyond all corporate or even national experience, the progress of the world illustrates the necessities and the uncertainties with which thought has to contend, and under the stress of which it must develop into policy and assert itself in conduct. This is, of course, an inevitable result of enlargement of scale, and the world movement presents action upon the greatest of all scales. There is vastly more of detail and of surprise, of the complicated and of the unexpected. Every nation or race deals with its own problems, — those of its internal and of its external life; but the fortune of each exerts a specific influence upon the general outcome. Not only are those influences very diverse in themselves, but they cause incessant change in the relations of the parts to each other and to the whole. Relative importance and the nature of that importance are subject to continual fluctuation. Enmities succeed to friendships; strength declines to weakness; accident, as men call it, in a moment and amid universal astonishment reverses conditions. Still, although liable at any moment to see hopes overthrown, combinations frustrated, and even the solidest foundations giving under their feet, nations and their rulers must take account of existing tendencies, argue from the present to the future, estimate the relative weight of contemporary factors, and from them forecast the probable issue, although it seem to lie beyond the horizon of their own generation; for in their day they are the guardians of posterity, and may not shirk their trust. They must, in short, take long views, and upon them in due measure act as opportunity permits; yet withal the uncertainties, both of calculations and of events, are so great, the difficulties of prediction and of speculation so obvious, that they are compelled to treat the situation of each moment in the light of immediate necessities, to take short views, to look primarily to their feet and to the next step, endeavoring only, if they may, that this be in the general direction which their practical sagacity has indicated as the far goal of the nation's good.

It would be an interesting study, but one quite apart from the object of this paper, to trace the genesis and evolution in the American people of the impulse towards expansion which has recently taken so decisive a stride. To do this adequately would involve the consideration of a volume of details, in order to extricate from them the leading features which characterize and demonstrate the vital sequence in the several stages of advance. The treatment of the matter, however, would be very imperfect if it failed clearly to recognize and to state that it is but one phase of a sentiment that has swept over the whole civilized European world within the last few decades, salient evidences of which are found in the advance of Russia in Asia, in the division of Africa, in the colonial ambitions of France and of Germany, in the naval growth of the latter, in the development of Japan, and in the British idea of Imperial Federation, now fast assuming concrete shape in practical combined action in South Africa. Every great state has borne its part in this common movement, the significance of which cannot be ignored. We may not know whence it comes nor whither it goes, but there it is. We see it and we hear it, and our own share in it has already radically changed our relations towards foreign states and races. Whatever its future, a future it clearly has, to read which men must lift up their hearts and strain their eyes, while at the same time they neglect not the present, but do with their might that which their hand at the moment finds to do.

A study of a particular phase of this possible future, as it appears to one man, is the object of this present paper. Before, however, proceeding with such consideration, it may be interesting, and not inappropriate, to note in briefest outline how singularly the long view and the short view have received illustration in the recent course of events. The intrinsic importance of Cuba, of the West Indies in general, and of the Isthmus of Panama, to the political, commercial, and military interests of the United States, was long ago perceived. To illustrate this by detailed account, from the words and actions of public men, would require an article — rather, perhaps, a volume — by itself; but it is easy to note, rising above the sea of incidental details, of diplomatic negotiations and governmental recommendations, a few landmarks, such as the Clayton-Bulwer Treaty, the attempt under Grant's administration to annex Santo Domingo, the abortive negotiations for the purchase of the Danish islands, our treaty with Colombia guaranteeing the transit of the Isthmus railway. Solicitude, which traced its origin to the early years of the century, increased to conviction as the expansion of the country emphasized the consciousness of a probable destiny. Deadened temporarily by the outbreak of the civil war, which it antedated by generations, it revived immediately upon its conclusion — the insistence upon the French withdrawal from Mexico being a first-fruits of quickened life. For the moment the long view had yielded to the imperious demands of the short; but, the emergency over, the nation again lifted its eyes and looked afar.

Meantime events had progressed and continued to progress. New factors had entered into the conditions, while the bearing and importance of old factors were seen more clearly and forcibly, for time had brought them out of the haze of distant speculation, and nearer to the decisive moment of action. The school of thought that looked to expansion became more incisive and outspoken, its ideas increasing in scope and in definiteness of expression. The long view, raising its vision gradually above the Antilles and the Isthmus, as these drew more into the foreground, saw beyond them the Pacific, Hawaii, and the beginning of momentous issues in China and Japan. There insight again was baffled; unless it may be claimed, as evidence of a wider range, that the country and the exponents of expansion, in common with the world at large, had at last aroused to consciousness of the determining influence of sea power upon the history of the world. Sea power, however, is but the handmaid of expansion, its begetter and preserver; it is not itself expansion, nor did the advocates of the latter foresee room for advance beyond the Pacific. Their vision reached not past Hawaii, which also, as touching the United States, they regarded from the point of view of defence rather than as a stepping-stone to any farther influence in the world. So far as came under the observation of the writer — and his interest in the matter dated back several years — the expansionists themselves, up to the war with Spain, were dominated by the purely defensive ideas inherited from the earlier days of our national existence. The Antilles, Cuba, the Isthmus, and Hawaii were up to that time simply outposts — positions — where it was increasingly evident that influences might be established dangerous to the United States as she then was. Such influences must be forestalled; if not by immediate action, at least by a definite policy.

It was to such a state of mind that the war with Spain came; and the result has the special interest of showing the almost instantaneous readiness with which a seed of thought germinates when it falls upon mental soil prepared already to receive it. Reflection and discussion, voice and pen, platform and press, had broken up the fallow ground left untilled by the generations which succeeded the fathers of the republic. Habit had familiarized men's minds with the idea of national power spreading beyond the bounds of this continent, and with the reasons that made it advisable, if not imperative. Though staggered for an instant by a proposition so entirely unexpected and novel as Asiatic dominion, the long view had done its work of preparation; and the short view, the action necessary at the minute, imposed primarily and inevitably by the circumstances of the instant, found no serious difficulty of acceptance, so far as concerned the annexation of the Philippines — the widest sweep, in space, of our national extension.

We have for the time being quite sufficient to occupy our activities in accommodating ourselves to these new conditions, and in organizing our duties under them. But while this is true as touching immediate action, it is not necessarily, nor equally, true as regards thought, directed upon the future. After a brief rest in contemplation of the present, effort must be resumed, not merely to note existing conditions, but to appreciate the tendencies involved in them — history in embryo — the issue of which will hereafter concern us or our descendants. Events of recent years have substantially changed the political relations of states, and thereby have imposed such a study of these as shall give point and direction to that long view of the distant future which, uncertain though it be in its calculations, and liable to sudden disconcertment, is nevertheless essential, if sagacious and continuous guidance is to be given to the course of a nation. Such study will require an intelligent and sustained resolution; for, with the possible exception of the Monroe doctrine, the people of the United

States have been by long habit indifferent to the subject of external policies. They have been so not only as the result of our particular circumstances of isolation, but by deliberate intention, inherited from a day when such abstinence was better justified than now, and depended upon a well-known, though misunderstood, warning of Washington against entangling alliances. Under changed conditions of the world, from the influence of which we cannot escape, it is imperative to arouse to the necessity of conscious effort, in order to recognize and to understand broad external problems, not merely as matters of general information or of speculative interest, but as questions in which we ourselves have, or may have, the gravest direct concern, as affecting ourselves or our children.

It is by such long views that is developed the readiness of decision, in unexpected conjunctures of international politics, which corresponds to presence of mind in common life; for ordinarily presence of mind means preparedness of mind, through previous reflection upon possible contingencies. The need of such readiness — of sustained apprehension of actual and of probable future conditions — receives the clearest demonstration from our recent experience. What more sudden or less expected, what, in a word, more illustrative of a short view resulting in decisive action, taken at a moment's notice, can be adduced than that a war begun with Spain about Cuba should result in tendering us the position of an Asiatic Power, with the consequent responsibilities and opportunities? Evidently a mind prepared by deliberation upon contemporary occurrences and tendencies is no mean equipment for prompt decision in such a case. It is in no wise a disconnected incident that the United States has been suddenly drawn out of her traditional attitude of apartness from the struggle of European states, and had a new element forced into her polity. The war with Spain has been but one of several events, nearly simultaneous, which have compelled mankind to fix their attention upon eastern Asia, and to realize that conditions there have so changed as to compel a readjustment of ideas, as well as of national policies and affiliations. Nothing is more calculated to impress the mind with the seriousness of the impending problems than the known fact that Japan, which less than four years ago notified our government of her disinclination to our annexation of Hawaii, now with satisfaction sees us in possession of the Philippines.

The altered conditions in the East have doubtless resulted — as did American expansion — from certain preparative antecedents, less obvious at the time of their occurrence, and which therefore then escaped particular notice; but the incidents that have signalized the change have been compacted into a very few years. Hence they possess the attribute of suddenness, which naturally entails for a time a lack of precise comprehension, with the necessary consequence of vagueness in opinion. Nevertheless, there they are; matters of grave international moment to those older nationalities, from whom heretofore we have held ourselves sedulously aloof. Side by side with them is our own acceptance of the Philippines, an act which we could not rightly avoid, and which carries with it opportunity. Opportunity, however, can never be severed from responsibility; for, whether utilized or neglected, a decision, positive or negative, is made, which cannot be dissociated from the imputation of moral right or wrong, of intellectual mistake or of wisdom.

It may be well here to consider for a moment the charge, now often made, that by the acceptance of the Philippines, and, still more, by any further use of the opportunities they may give us, we abandon the Monroe doctrine. The argument, if it can be allowed that name, derives such force as it has from appeal to prejudice; a word which, although it has an invidious association, does not necessarily imply more than opinion already formed, and which, if resting on solid basis, is entitled to full respect, unless, and until, it refuses to face new conditions. The Monroe doctrine, however, commits us only to a national policy, which may be comprehensively summarized as an avowed purpose to resist the extension of the European system to the American continents. As a just counterweight to this pretension, which rests in no wise upon international law, but upon our own interests as we understand them, we have adopted, as a rule of action, abstention from interference — even by suggestion, and much more by act — in questions purely European.

Of these complementary positions, neither the one nor the other possesses any legal standing, any binding force, of compact or of precedent. We are at liberty to abandon either at once, without incurring any just imputation of unlawful action. Regarded, however, purely as a matter of policy, and as such accepted as wise, by what process of reasoning is it to be established that either the one rule or the other bars us, on the ground of consistency, from asserting what we think our rights in Asia? In its inception the Monroe doctrine was, I suppose, a recognition of the familiar maxim of statesmen that geographical propinquity is a source of trouble between nations, which we, being favored by natural isolation, proposed to avert; and to this proposition the determination to keep clear of questions internal to Europe was an inevitable corollary. We took advantage, in short, of an opportunity extended to us by fortunate conditions to assure our national quiet. But there are provinces other than geographical in which the interests of nations approach and mingle, and in those we have never been deterred by the Monroe doctrine from acting as our duties or our interests demanded. It has never, that I know, been seriously wished to compass our ends by the acquisition of European territory, for it would be neither expedient nor justifiable, even if possible, to unsettle conditions the permanency of which is the secure evolution of centuries of racial and national history; but we have had no scruples of justice or of expediency as to extension of territory in this hemisphere, where no such final 'adjustments had been reached. Now in Asia we are confronted at this moment by questions in which our interests will probably be largely involved. There is no more inconsistency in taking there such action as the case demands than there has been in any international difference we have hitherto had with a European power; while if such action should involve use of territory, directly or incidentally, by possession or by control — sphere of influence — it will only be because decadent conditions there shall hereafter have resulted in a lack of power, either to perpetuate a present system or to resist encroachments which the progress of the world under the impulse of more virile states is sure to entail. There is certainly no desire, but rather unwillingness, on the part of the United States to undertake such an addition to her responsibilities, otherwise sufficiently great; both her traditions and her present policy are necessarily adverse to such action. Still it must be considered as a possible contingency, however deplorable, for, if life departs, a carcass can be utilized only by dissection or for food; the gathering to it of the eagles is a natural law, of which it is bootless to complain. The onward movement of the world has to be accepted as a fact, to be advantageously dealt with by guidance, not by mere opposition, still less by unprofitable bewailing of things irretrievably past.

The Monroe doctrine has been and continues to be a good serviceable working theory, resting on undeniable conditions. But, having now a lifetime of several generations, it has acquired an added force of tradition, of simple conservatism, which has a bad as well as a good side. For tradition tends to invest accepted policy with the attribute of permanency, which only exceptionally can be predicated of the circumstances of this changing world. The principles upon which an idea rests may conform to essential, and therefore permanent, truth; but application continually varies, and maxims, rules, doctrines, not being the living breath of principles, but only their embodiment — the temporary application of them to conditions not necessarily permanent — can claim no exemption from the ebb and flow of mundane things. We should not make of even this revered doctrine a fetich, nor persuade ourselves that a modification is under no circumstances admissible.

For instance, it has become probable that, whatever our continued adherence to the doctrine itself, we may have somewhat to readjust our views of its corollary — that concerning apartness from European complications. It is not, indeed, likely, in any view that can be taken within our present horizon, that we should find reason for intervention in a dispute localized in Europe itself; but it is nevertheless most probable that we can never again see with indifference, and with the sense of security which characterized our past, a substantial, and still less a radical, change in the balance of power there. The progress of the world has brought us to a period when it is well within the range of possibilities that the declension of a European state might immediately and directly endanger our own interests; might involve us in action, either to avert the catastrophe itself or to remedy its consequences. From this follows the obvious necessity of appreciating the relations to ourselves of the power inherent in various countries, due to their available strength and to their position; what also their attitude towards us, resultant from the temper of the people, and the intelligent control of the latter by the government — two very different things, even in democratic communities. Herein, again, we only share the common fate of all nations; for not only do all touch one another more closely than of old, but — and especially in Asia — conditions external to all are drawing the regard of all towards a common centre, where as yet nothing certain is determined, where the possibilities of the future are many, and diverse, and great.

In so large a question as the future of Asia, upon which are now converging, from many quarters, streams of influence representing the interests, not of nationalities only, but of the larger groups which we know as races, it is well to study first the broad geographical features, in their several attributes — such as disposition, area, physical characteristics, distances — and thereafter the present political distribution, with the possibilities which result from both. To these considerations, pertaining to the continent itself, must be added an appreciation of the environing circumstances, even if distant, which are involved in the territorial situation of other nations, Asiatic or European; in their relative strength and its kinds — political, economical, military, naval; in their readiness of access to the continent of Asia — the length, nature, and facilities of the communications to and fro; the Asiatic positions, if such there be, now held by them — secondary bases, whence their influence, political or military, may be brought to bear. For the problem of Asia is a world problem, which has come upon the world in an age when, through the rapidity of communication, it is wide awake and sensible as never before, and by electrical touch, to every stirring in its members, and to the tendency thereof. But sensitiveness is not the same thing as understanding, any more than symptoms are identical with diagnosis. Study is requisite; and as a preliminary it may be observed that political problems into which the element of geography enters have much in common with military strategy. There will be found in both a centre of interest — an objective; the positions of the parties concerned, which are the bases of their strength and operations, even when these are peaceful; and there is the ability to project their power to the centre of interest, which answers to the communications that play so leading a part in military art, because power that cannot be transmitted freely ceases in so far to be operative power. It is, in fact, this quality, facility of transmission, that has made sea power so multifold in manifestation and in efficiency.

As we look at the continent of Asia, in its length and breadth, we may note, first, that it lies wholly north of the equator, and in great part between the northern tropic and the arctic circle — that is, in the so-called temperate zone. The inferences as to climate which might be drawn from this are deceptive, owing to modifications occasioned by physical conditions. The great plains of the north and of the south — of Siberia and of India — are subject, respectively, to extremes of cold and of heat, due primarily to the vast extent of land in the continent itself, which precludes the moderating power of the sea from exercising extensive influence. The effect of this immense region upon temperature is most strikingly shown in the monsoons, the periodical winds which alternate with the seasons — as land and sea breezes change with night and day — but which during their continuance have the steadiness characteristic of the permanent trades. This phenomenon, which prevails throughout the Indian Ocean, the Bay of Bengal, and the China

Sea, is attributable to the alternate heating and cooling of the continent, as the sun moves north or south of the equator, inducing a periodical set of the atmosphere — from the northeast during the winter, and from the southwest during the summer.

Within its main outlines, the greatest breadth of the continent from east to west is about five thousand statute miles, following the thirtieth degree of north latitude; but along the fortieth this distance is increased by some hundreds of miles, through the projection of two peninsulas — Asia Minor on the west, and Korea on the east. Between these two parallels are to be found, speaking roughly, the most decisive natural features, and also those political divisions the unsettled character of which renders the problem of Asia in the present day at once perplexing and imminent. Within this belt are the Isthmus of Suez, Palestine and Syria, Mesopotamia, the greater part of Persia, and Afghanistan — with the strong mountain ranges that mark these two countries and Armenia — the Pamir, the huge elevations of Tibet, and a large part of the valley of the Yang-tse-kiang, with the lower and most important thousand miles of that river's course.

Within it also are the cities of Aleppo, Mosul, and Bagdad, of Teheran and Ispahan, of Merv and Herat, Kabul and Kandahar, and in the far east of China, Peking, Shanghai, Nanking, and Han-kow. No one of these is in the territory of a state the stability of which can be said to repose securely upon its own strength, or even upon the certainty of non-interference by ambitious neighbors. The chain of the Himalayas is exterior to, but only a little south of, the zone indicated. Although Japan is extra-continental, it may be interesting to note that the greater part of her territory and the centre of her power lie also within the belt, and extend almost across it, from north to south.

Within these bounds, speaking broadly and not exclusively, is the debatable and debated ground. North and south of it, in similar wide generalization, political conditions are relatively determined, though by no means absolutely fixed. Along the northern and southern borders, where exterior impulses impinge, there are uncertainty and jealousy, aggression and defence, not as yet military, but political. Still, whatever its form, such action is at bottom that of conflicting, if not contending, impulses. The division of Asia is east and west; movement is north and south. It is the character of that movement, and its probable future, as indicated by the relative forces, and by the lines which in physics are called those of least resistance, that we are called to study; for in the greatness of the stake, and in the relative settledness of conditions elsewhere, there is assurance that there will continue to be motion until an adjustment is reached, either in the satisfaction of everybody, or by the definite supremacy of some one of the contestants. Practically, if not logically, equilibrium may consist in decisive overweight, as well as in an even balance — another paradoxical truth.

That the dividing line of unsettled political status is along the belt defined may be ascertained by a brief examination of a map. That movement is from and to the north and the south is a matter of history — not yet a generation old — and of names familiar to all readers of news. The mere sound of Turkestan, Khiva, Merv, Herat, Kandahar, Kabul, attests the fact; as do Manchuria and Port Arthur. Thus both in the western half and in the extreme east is observed the same tendency, which would be still more amply demonstrated by an appeal to history but little more remote. It is, in fact, no longer consistent with accuracy of forecast to draw a north and south line of severance; to contemplate eastern Asia apart from western; to dissociate, practically, the conditions and incidents in the one from those in the other. Both form living parts of a large problem, to which both contribute elements of perplexity. The relations of each to the other, and to the whole, must therefore be considered.

Accepting provisionally the east and west belt of division as one stage in the process of analysis, we may profitably consider next the character and distribution of the forces whose northward and southward impulses constitute the primary factors in the process of change already initiated and still continuing. Upon a glance at the map one enormous fact immediately obtrudes itself upon the attention — the vast, uninterrupted mass of the Russian Empire, stretching without a break in territorial consecutiveness from the meridian of western Asia Minor, until to the eastward it overpasses that of Japan. In this huge distance no political obstacles intervene to impede the concentrated action of the disposable strength. Within the dominion of Russia only the distances themselves, and the hindrances — unquestionably great and manifold — imposed by natural conditions, place checks upon her freedom and fulness of movement. To this element of power — central position — is to be added the wedge-shaped outline of her territorial projection into central Asia, strongly supported as this is, on the one flank, by the mountains of the Caucasus and the inland Caspian Sea — wholly under her control — and on the other by the ranges which extend from Afghanistan, northeasterly, along the western frontier of China. From the latter, moreover, she as yet has no serious danger to fear.

The fact of her general advance up to the present time, most of which has been made within a generation, so that the point of the wedge is now inserted between Afghanistan and Persia, must be viewed in connection with the tempting relative facility of farther progress through Persia to the Persian Gulf, and with the strictly analogous movement, on the other side of the continent, where long strides have been made through Manchuria to Port Arthur and the Gulf of Pe-chi-li. Thus, alike in the far east and in the far west, we find the same characteristic of remorseless energy, rather remittent than intermittent in its symptoms. Russia, in obedience to natural law and race instinct, is working, geographically, to the southward in Asia by both flanks, her centre covered by the mountains of Afghanistan and the deserts of eastern Turkestan and Mongolia. Nor is it possible, even if it were desired, to interfere with the internal action, the mutual support, of the various sections of this extended line, whose length under the physical and political conditions is less an element of weakness; for the Russian centre cannot be broken. It is upon, and from, the flanks of this great line that restraint, if needed, must come; the opposition of those who, with no ill-will to Russia, no grudging of her prosperity, nevertheless think that undue predominance is an unsound condition in any body politic — in the parliament of man, if we may say so, as well as in that of a nation. In the federation of the world, if it ever come to pass, healthy politics will need an opposition of parties, drawn doubtless along national or racial lines.

As north and south are logically opposed, so it might be surmised that practically the opposition to this movement of Russia from the north would find its chief expression to the south of the broad dividing belt, between the thirtieth and fortieth parallels. In a measure this is so, but with a very marked distinction, not only in degree but in kind. In the progress of history, in which, as it unrolls, more and more of plan and of purpose seems to become evident, the great central peninsula of southern Asia, also projecting wedge-shaped far north into the middle debatable zone, has come under the control of a people the heart of whose power is far removed from it locally, and who, to the concentration of territory characteristic of Russia's geographical position, present an extreme of racial and military dispersal. India, therefore, is to Great Britain not the primary base of operations, political and military — for military action is only a specialized form of political. It is simply one of many contingent — secondary — bases, in different parts of the world, the action of which is susceptible of unification only by means of a supreme sea power. Of these many bases, India is the one best fitted, by nearness and by conformation, both for effect upon Central Asia and for operations upon either extremity of the long line over which the Russian front extends. Protected on the land side and centre by the mountains of Afghanistan and the

Himalayas, its flanks, thrown to the rear, are unassailable, so long as the navy remains predominant. They constitute also frontiers, from which, in the future as in the past, expeditions may make a refreshed and final start, for Egypt on the one hand, for China on the other; and, it is needless to add, for any less distant destination in either direction.

It is not intrinsically only that India possesses the value of a base to Great Britain. The central position which she holds relatively to China and to Egypt obtains also towards Australia and the Cape of Good Hope, assisting thus the concentration upon her of such support as either colony can extend to the general policy of an Imperial Federation. Even in its immediate relations to Asiatic problems, however, India is not unsupported. On land and in the centre, the acquisition of Burmah gives a continuous extension of frontier to the east, which turns the range of the Himalayas, opening access, political or peaceful, for influence or for commerce, to the upper valley of the Yang-tse-kiang, and to the western provinces of China proper. By sea, the Straits Settlements and Hong-kong on the one side, Aden and Egypt on the other, faciliate, as far as land positions can, maritime enterprises to the eastward or to the westward, directed in a broad sense upon the flanks of the dividing zone, or upon those of the opposing fronts of operations that mark the deployment of the northern and southern powers, which at the present time are most strongly established upon Asian territory.

The British and Russian territorial developments in Asia, as thus summarized, constitute the local bases, upon which depend not merely movement, peaceful or warlike, if such take place, but the impulse to action, defensive or offensive, felt by either nation. Were they not where they are, much that now engages their attention would pass unremarked; but, being there, there arise from the positions exterior opportunities and dangers, which neither state should nor can neglect. It becomes therefore necessary to consider, and to summarize, what those dangers and opportunities are; for they constitute the external interests, which in the political field correspond to the objectives of strategy in the Art of War.

The first law of states, as of men, is self-preservation — a term which cannot be narrowed to the bare tenure of a stationary round of existence.

Growth is a property of healthful life, which does not, it is true, necessarily imply increase of size for nations, any more than it does for individuals, with whom bodily, and still more mental, development progresses long after stature has reached its limit; but it does involve the right to insure by just means whatsoever contributes to national progress, and correlatively to combat injurious action taken by an outside agency, if the latter overpass its own lawful sphere. When a difference between two states can be brought to the test of ascertained and defined right, this carries with it a strong presumption in favor of submission; but when a matter touches only advantage, not qualified by law or by prescription, and the question therefore is one of expediency, it is justly and profitably considered in the light of self-preservation. This includes the right of growth, common to both, which is not legal but natural, and consequently less capable of precise definition. It is a great gain, not only to the parties concerned, but to mankind at large, when each candidly regards in this light the claims of an opponent as well as its own, and seeks to strike a fair balance by mutual concession or impartial arbitration; but it still remains true that in such a transaction governments — and even nations — are not principals, but agents, having in charge that which is not their own, but their trust, for the generation that then is and for those which are to follow. Relinquishment, therefore, and recourse to arbitration, are conditioned by the element of trusteeship, and cannot be embraced in that spirit of simple self-sacrifice which is so admirable in the individual man dealing with what is wholly his own.

It is therefore not enough to direct attention to the security, in territorial tenure, of the two parties who at the present moment are the principal exponents of the contending impulses in Asia. There must be considered also the need and right to grow, as these may be affected either by their own opposing tendencies, or by conditions now existing in Asia itself, and localized for the most part in the dividing belt of debatable ground. Nor can the question be confined to the two most prominent disputants. The right to grow, of the world in general, and of other states in particular, is involved in these Asian problems, in the development and utilization of this vast tract, so long isolated from a share in the general order.

Growth depends upon two correlative factors; upon vigor of internal organization — which gives power to assimilate — and upon freedom of interchange with external sources of support. In the family of civilized states, the former is solely the concern of the nation itself; intervention from without, in the internal order of a community, is generally held to be permissible only when its stage of political development corresponds to that of childhood or of decay. The matter, in fact, is one properly and naturally internal, only exceptionally and accidentally one for interference from outside. It is quite different with freedom of interchange; for that, depending upon conditions external to the country, implies necessarily external acquiescence, both of the people with whom interchange is had, and of those whose interests are involved in the intervening channels of communication.

The methods of the British or Russian internal administration are therefore outside of such a discussion as this, except in so far as they indicate the probable effect upon other countries of the extension of these methods to territory desired, but not yet obtained. This is, indeed, a most serious consideration, and one that cannot fail to weigh heavily in the determination of policies. The ubiquitous tendency to territorial expansion, which is so marked a feature in European states of the period, results in a corresponding contraction of the ground free equally to all; and, as this narrows, there cannot but be increasing jealousy of every movement which carries a threat of exclusive control, whether by acquisition or by predominant influence, especially if the latter depend not upon fair commercial struggle in open markets, but upon the alien element of military or political force.

Whatever, therefore, may be the commercial possibilities involved in the application of modern methods to the further development of the countries and peoples which lie between the zones of British and Russian power in Asia, one single interest will be common to all the nations who seek by commerce — by interchange — to promote their own healthy national growth. Each alike will desire that it, individually, have its equal chance in the field, unhindered by the inimical influence of a foreign power, resting not upon fair competition, but upon force, whether exerted by open act or by secret pressure. Nothing is more dreaded, nor will be more resented

— more productive of quarrel — than such interposition. In the final analysis the question is as yet essentially military. Time, much time, will be needed for the process of development; but the movement is already in progress through which, by the acquisition of new positions, and by the consolidation of power both in them and in territory already held, advantage will be gained for the exercise of control.

What has just been said applies to all the belt lying, roughly, between the thirtieth and fortieth parallels, and not to China only, although the latter, through her huge area and population, and her seeming helplessness, has naturally attracted the greater attention. The question also is, for the present, quite independent of the aggregate results of development, which not impossibly may fall very short of the rosy hopes of trade suggested by the mere words "four hundred millions of people." Those results, being so far in the future as to defy exact prediction, affect the question much as a variable quantity does a mathematical problem — that is, not at all, so far as the process of investigation is concerned, the effect being shown only when different values are assigned to it in the final expression. Be that variable quantity — the result of development — great or small, its possibilities are great, and as such it must be taken into account in discussing the political problem of obviating *now* the chance of any exclusive, or unduly preponderant, usufruct *then*.

On this account, in regarding the central zone of Asia as a source whence the nations of the world, by mutual exchange or benefit, can both invigorate their own life and that of the Asiatics, it seems quite just and reasonable to discard all attempt to estimate by detail how abundant that source may prove to be. Even if utilization be confined to the labor and capital employed in developing internal communications, the mutual effect will be great enough to merit consideration. How much more the future may hold is indifferent to the necessary forecast — the short view — of the present. The problem, into the final solution of which enter all the factors — military and naval power, military and naval positions, communications external and internal, commercial operations and benefits — is less one of proportion than of scale; and the scale will depend upon the value of that unknown and variable quantity, the potential wealth of the countries concerned, when they shall have become fully developed members of the international body.

The contribution, direct and indirect, which these regions may eventually make to the general prosperity of the world is the substantial interest which is now attracting the attention of the nations. From their aim to control or to share it, it corresponds to the objective of strategy in military operations. Accepting provisionally the conclusion just reached as to its present indeterminate value, we have next to consider the question of approaches from without, which in their turn answer to the communications that play so leading a part in the policy of war. Communications that are wholly internal fall into the category of commercial development, except where they may form sections of a great international line.

It will be apparent at once that communications — approaches from without — are of two chief kinds — by sea and by land. In these heads of division they recall the essential differences between the two European powers now most solidly settled on Asiatic soil. These concurrent facts — and factors — suggest, what will hereafter become increasingly apparent, that we have here again a fresh instance of the multiform struggle between land power and sea power. Consequently, it is not improbable that the recognition and constant recollection of this perennial contest may serve better than any other clew to guide us through this complicated inquiry, and to reach an adjustment between the two antagonists that can most certainly and most easily be maintained. Such an adjustment would be one in which the respective aggregates of power, whatever its component parts on either side, should approach equality, in amount and in disposition, while causes of friction should at the same time be minimized. If these two conditions — the smallest friction, and equality of power — be insured, there will follow from them the least disposition to break the peace.

Lines of communication by sea, whatever their starting-point and their course, extend as far as ships can float and navigate. So far they exist independent of man's power, which does not determine their existence, but the use of them. In copiousness they exceed, irretrievably, the utmost possibilities of land travel. This is consequent, partly, upon the greater obstacles to transit imposed by the ground under its most favorable conditions, and partly upon the undue expense incurred, owing to the same obstacles, in attempting by increase of width, or by multiplication of tracks, to rival the expanses of water routes. As a highway, a railroad competes in vain with a river — the greater speed cannot compensate for the smaller carriage. Because more facile and more copious, water traffic is for equal distances much cheaper; and, because cheaper, more useful in general. These distinctions are not accidental or temporary; they are of the nature of things, and permanent. Only where there is no water communication, or when excess of distance by water as compared with that by land counterbalances the intrinsic advantages of the former, can there be competition in cheapness and in generalness of use. It is necessary to insist upon these facts; for the far greater speed of the railroad gives a very different impression to the average mind, which is prone to forget the limitations in capacity. Traffic, or exchange of goods, depends in aggregate result not upon speed only but upon the amounts that can be steadily delivered in long equal periods of time.

These inherent advantages of water communications will probably insure their preponderance, in exploiting the development of the regions now under consideration. But, as has before been observed, the existence of sea communications is one thing; the use of them is another. The latter depends upon power, and that power manifested in two ways, namely, by pure naval strength upon the ocean, and by a combination — or conflict, it may be — of naval and military strength, where the ocean touches or penetrates the land. There, where they meet, opposition on the score of military power, which underlies political power, is of course accentuated, and the balance must be determined. Such local determination, however, does not affect merely the neighborhood in which it is exerted. The nature, extent, and decisiveness of territorial control, established by power resting upon the sea, constitute a centre of political influence, corresponding to a base of military operations, from which are radiated effects which reach far inland, and exert a force commensurate in diffusion and in degree to that of the base from which they issue.

Thus land power is modified by the proximity

of the sea; and correspondingly, whenever the ocean touches the land, the circumstance at once conditions sea power, which no longer represents a single factor, but becomes a resultant, dependent in character upon the contrasted strengths of opposing forces. This is seen, in different phases and degrees, in the entrances of seaports and of navigable rivers; in the ascent of the latter; in the effect of islands as well as of coastlines upon strategy; in straits such as Gibraltar, or canals like Suez. In all these cases the power of the land to interfere with that of the sea is easily obvious. It is seen again, in the most extreme form, where an international water route is interrupted, as at the Isthmus of Panama, by land transit — like the portage between two inlands streams — or where, from the close approach of the land, such interruption can readily be caused. This liability naturally is greatest with artificial water routes, of which the Suez Canal is the most conspicuous existing example; but it would receive illustration also in the case of a railway from the Mediterranean to the Persian Gulf, which undoubtedly will be a feature of the future development of Asia.

Considering the respective prerogatives of the

land and of the sea, regarded as channels of communication, and their mutual influence when in contact, there can be little doubt that with China, as with other countries that enjoy a sea frontier, the latter will be the more fruitful medium of promoting commerce — the interchange — whereby nations in vigorous life sustain and develop their strength through contact with outside sources, which, in return, are thus not exhausted, but renewed. This general tendency will receive special impulse and force from the Yang-tse-kiang, which, being navigable by steamers a thousand miles from its mouth, extends so far the access from the sea to the heart of this great valley of China. And as with the country possessing the seaboard, so with those whose approach to her is through it, and by the sea. The greater ease, and therefore the greater copiousness, of the stream of traffic result in a corresponding increase in the wealth — the gain — which is the concrete expression of the mutual benefit. Greater benefit entails greater interest — interest in the maintenance and promotion of the more favorable conditions; that is, those who are deriving the largest good from the exchange — from commerce — will be most anxious to continue and to develop it, and, as commerce thrives by peace and suffers by war, it follows that peace is the superior interest of those countries which approach by the sea. It is, indeed, a reiterated commonplace that the interest of a commercial state is peace. Such countries will indeed need to support their policy of peace by readiness to resort to war if need be; but locally such military preparation as they may have will be essentially defensive, not aggressive. This results also from another cause; for, while they have the greater interest and the stronger control — one approaching, in fact, to decisiveness — over the sea communications, their power of territorial control cannot directly outweigh that of a state whose frontiers are conterminous with the region in dispute. It is this limited capacity of navies to extend coercive force inland that has commended them to the highest political intelligence, as a military instrument mighty for defence, but presenting no menace to the liberties of a people.

The distribution of the Russian dominion and the concentration of its mass, already alluded to, combined with the fact of its irremediable remoteness from an open sea, render inevitable its dependence upon land routes for the bulk of its intercourse with the debatable ground of Asia. Natural conditions are so hopelessly adverse, that it is difficult to see what possible political extension can seriously modify them. By this is meant that, wherever Russia now touches the sea, or can shortly touch it, the points are so remote from the heart of her territory that access to it from them must, after all, be chiefly by land. The benefit of sea commerce, therefore, will extend from her seaboard only to a distance short relatively to the extent of the empire; while the localities immediately benefited are comparatively small, and not especially adapted to those forms of development which sea commerce promotes. They have the further disadvantage that they are upon enclosed seas, liable, therefore, to be definitively shut by a hostile power — land or sea, as the case may be. It is sufficient merely to glance at the Dardanelles and the approaches to the Baltic to see the force of this remark.

From these conditions it results that, if the comparative advantages and results of land and water traffic are as has been stated above, Russia is in a disadvantageous position for the accumulation of wealth; which is but another way of saying that she is deficient in means for advancing the welfare of her people, of which wealth is at once the instrument and the exponent. This being so, it is natural and proper that she should be dissatisfied, and dissatisfaction readily takes the form of aggression — the word most in favor with those of us who dislike all forward movement in nations. Her tendency necessarily must be to advance, and it is already sufficiently pronounced to be suggestive of ultimate aims. It would be a curious speculation to consider how far the systematic forward designs often attributed to her, as in the rumored will of Peter the Great, simply reflect the universal consciousness of her evident needs and consequent restlessness. This is possibly the largest single element in the horoscope of Asia, and it may be stated thus: Only parts of the Russian territory, and those, even in the aggregate, small and uninfluential comparatively to the whole, enjoy the benefits of maritime commerce. It is therefore the interest of Russia not merely to reach the sea at more points, and more independently, but to acquire, by possession or by control, the usufruct of other and extensive maritime regions, the returns from which shall redound to the general prosperity of the entire empire. To this statement must necessarily be added the consideration of those peculiarities of Russian internal administration and general policy, which, after annexation, tend to the substantial exclusion of other states from much that they have enjoyed prior to Russian occupation.

It is a mistake, and a deplorable mistake, when recognizing conditions of conflicting interests, as here indicated, to see in them only grounds for opposition and hostility. States that are more fortunate in the extent of their seaboard, and in physical conditions which facilitate the circulation of the life-blood of trade throughout their organization, owe at the least candor, if not sympathy, to the fetters under which Russia labors in her narrow sea-front, in her vast and difficult interior, and in a climate of extreme rigor.

Nevertheless, while such an attitude should be observed and maintained, there remains the duty to their own people; and associated with these, but dominating both, the moral obligations to the populations and to the governments still more immediately concerned — those of the debatable zone — in changes which seem impending. We are not in the presence of a simple problem, easily decided by reference merely to existing rights — natural, prescriptive, or legal — or to the firmly established principles of a highly developed society of individuals or of nations. We are confronted with the imminent dissolution of one or more organisms, or with a readjustment of their parts, the results of which, should either come to pass, will be solid and durable just in proportion as the existence and force of natural factors either are accurately recognized, or else reach an equilibrium by free self-assertion, allowing each to find its proper place through natural selection. Such a struggle, however, as is implied in the phrase "natural selection," involves conflict and suffering that might be avoided, in part at least, by the rational process of estimating the forces at work, and approximating to the natural adjustment by the artificial methods of counsel and agreement, which seem somewhat more suitable to the present day.

CHAPTER II

IN the relation of land power to the future of Middle Asia — between the parallels of thirty and forty north — natural conditions have bestowed upon Russia a pre-eminence which approaches exclusiveness. The share of other states, where any exists, is incidental; and with one conspicuous exception, which will be indicated later, is deficient either in numbers, position, or organization. This predominance will enable Russia to put forth her strength unopposed, directly, by any other of the same nature, in quarters outside of the extreme range that can with any probability be predicated of sea power. But where immediate opposition is not feasible, adequate restraint is frequently imposed by force exerted, or capable of exertion, in other quarters, by land or by sea — dependent, as all force is, partly upon its own intrinsic value and partly upon positions occupied. Such pressure is possible, more or less, in all conditions of life, where interests are extensive, various, or scattered. It is notably so in international life, where action in one quarter is continually hindered by the consciousness of weakness elsewhere. Brought into action for military ends, this means of constraint is known technically as " diversion."

To distraction and enfeeblement of this kind, should cause be given by the pursuance of a policy too selfishly exclusive, Russia is particularly liable, from her vast extent, inadequate internal communications, the number and power of the nations whose interests will suffer from such exclusion, and from the very favorable positions occupied by them for action that falls under the general head of diversion. The facility for this is the greater because the positions thus occupied, or open to occupation upon advantageous terms, are upon the Russian flanks, and, other things approaching equality, pressure or attack of a given amount upon a flank is applied to greater effect than upon the centre of a line, for the simple reason that each flank is more remote from the other than the centre is from either; concentration of effort, offensive or defensive, therefore, is more easily practised between the centre and a flank than between the flanks themselves. So many and great, indeed, are the opportunities of opposing states, due to position and strength, that, after all allowance made for the feebleness of alliances, or rather of co-operation, when compared with force concentrated in a single hand, it may still be believed that in potentiality the land and sea powers approach that condition of equilibrium which has been mentioned as one of the two factors that will tend to promote a peaceful and durable solution of the problem of Asia.

Unhappily the other factor, freedom from friction, is now conspicuous chiefly by its absence. Without attempting to pronounce upon the reasonableness of the feeling, it may safely be said that uneasiness, which is the mental equivalent of friction, is now notoriously prevalent in the councils of nations. In order that the worst result of such uneasiness — war — may be timely and effectually averted, a general appreciation of the conditions, and of the attitude necessary to be taken, is indispensable. Failing that, nations drift. Through ignorance of their strength and of their weakness, of the strength and weakness of those opposed to them, and of the elements in which strength or weakness consists, states and governments hesitate to act when action is opportune, are hasty when time is not ripe. In either case they act amiss, and incur danger, less or more; whereas, when thoroughly aroused to facts as they actually are, to the possibilities which they contain, and attentive to the preparations which circumstances demand, the common readiness and resulting mutual respect promote a measuredness and precision of action that more than aught else tend to preserve peace, by forestalling the occurrence of situations whence there is no escape but by war. It is doubtless this appreciation of relative powers and positions, joined to care so to maintain their own as to render a conflict arduous, even if not of uncertain issue, that now most effectually preserves peace among the states of Europe.

In like manner the nations closely concerned in the future of Asia — using the name in the broad sense that shall cover the entire continent — will most surely reach a solution of peace by a rational valuation of present advantages and disadvantages, of the interests at stake, and of the combinations possible, in the East; and then by making provision, corresponding to their necessities and resources, and to their numbers and positions, as shown by these calculations. Thus will result an adjustment of power answering to the facts of the case, and a mutual understanding, tacit rather than expressed: conditions which are the logical opposites of friction and uneasiness, and which, as they already do in Europe itself, will avert war and preserve a healthy balance of control in these remote scenes of conflicting aspirations. Similarly, in this our study, having estimated the opportunities and drawbacks inherent in the position of Russia, we have next to consider those of the states which would naturally operate as checks upon her too exclusive predominance. In doing this, incidental account of course must be taken, not only of natural conditions, but of the artificial combinations, or alliances, which notoriously exist. The wisdom of the latter, as corresponding to a real national interest, is not here in question; with such facts we have to deal simply as they are.

Among the means of successful diversion which natural conditions put in the hands of sea power, the control of commerce is probably the most decisive. It corresponds to, and counterbalances, that exclusiveness of command which land power has over the interior of countries inaccessible to navigation; nor is there, upon the face of the deep, the home and realm of sea power, any other equivalent compensation for this exclusion from the land. In itself the sea is a barren tenure; only as the great common, the highway of commerce, the seat of communications, does it possess unique character and value. The concrete expression of this singular importance of the sea is the merchandise in transit, the increment from which constitutes the material prosperity of nations. Surrender control of that, and the empire of the sea is like unto Samson shorn of his hair. It becomes the sea powers, therefore, in view of the solidarity of their interest in the approaching future, to consider seriously how far they will yield to the cry, now increasingly popular, for loosing the hold which, when belligerents, they have heretofore had over commerce in its broader sense. In view of the limitation of their means, otherwise, for enforcing their necessary policy, they should at least delay, and maturely weigh the general question, before, in deference to supposed particular advantage, they pledge themselves antecedently to the greater immunities now clamorously demanded.

Time should be taken before signing away prerogatives sanctioned by long prescription, such as the seizure of so-called private property, embarked on mercantile venture: the claim of which to the title "private" is open to grave challenge. The acceptance of precise definitions upon a subject essentially so variable in its character as contraband of war is also to be deprecated; nor would it be amiss, while thus studying the whole subject, to review, in the light of the probable future, the concession that, on the sea, enemy's goods are covered by the neutral flag — a maxim which the eminent Liberal statesman Charles Fox said was "neither good law nor good sense." The empire of the sea is doubtless the empire of the world; doubtless also its sceptre can be abdicated; but is it wise to do so?

Merchandize belonging to private individuals, but in transit to other countries for commercial exchange, is not "private" property in the ordinary sense of the word. It is a commonplace that money is the sinews of war. When embarked in foreign trade, the merchandize of individual citizens is engaged in making money for the state; it plays a most important part in the circulation of the life-blood throughout the organization of the belligerent country. It differs essentially from internal trade. The latter, coming from and returning to the nation itself, excluding other states in its course, resembles merely the functional activities of the animal body, which distribute to the various parts only that which the body already possesses. The body does not — cannot — live off itself; it simply assimilates and distributes that which it receives from outside, and this indispensable external nutriment corresponds to external commerce in the body political and economical, drawing support to the state from outside sources. From these sources, maritime commerce is the great channel of communication; hence its supreme importance to the support of war. To interrupt internal trade produces derangement of functional processes, which may conduce to the end of a war, or may not. If it does not so conduce, it stands condemned as causing useless suffering. As to the stoppage of external commerce, by capturing the so-called "private" property embarked, there can be no doubt about the effect. It conduces directly to the ends of war by producing a bloodless exhaustion, compelling submission, and that at the least expense of life and suffering.

It has been said that, viewing Russia as a whole, relatively to the middle zone of Asia, her advance has been, and promises still to be, by the flanks rather than by the centre. Such certainly are the present tendencies and indications. It is upon the flanks also, and upon the flanks chiefly, that opposition can be effectually made; but such opposition will be of the most forcible character, not only on account of the advantage already stated, inherent to flank attacks generally, but because it will be upon the line of the sea frontier — the seaboard — and accordingly upon the access to the sea, with which the interior, for its best welfare, requires untrammelled communication. It will be also in the hands of powers which, by the nature of their strength, and by their local positions in Asia, are essentially powers of the sea.

Let us, then, examine the conditions upon the flanks: first, as involving objects of interest — objectives of policy — control of which may be coveted; and secondly, with reference to the positions — the local tenure — of the states which may be aiming there to exert influence, whether for advance or for its prevention, and to their intrinsic strength for such purposes.

Accepting the estimates already made of Russia's position and necessary aims, her interests may be condensed into access to the sea as extensive and as free as possible: on the east by the Chinese seaboard; on the west in two directions, viz., to the Persian Gulf, by way of Persia, and to the Mediterranean, from the Black Sea, or through Asia Minor. Such plans are deducible, not from knowledge of the councils of the Russian government, but from the history of the recent past, and from the clear natural conditions indicating the lines which offer least resistance to forward movement, whether in the physical obstacles to be overcome, or in the opposition of the populations. It is allowable to add to these conjectured projects the common surmise of Russian design upon India. This, if entertained, would be an advance by the centre rather than by a flank; but even here a study of the map would seem to show that progress through Persia would not only approach the gulf, but if successful would turn — would outflank — the mountains of Afghanistan, avoiding the difficulties presented by the severe features of that country and by the character of its inhabitants. Russia would thus obtain a better position, both in itself and in its communication with the north, for beginning and sustaining operations in India itself.

Such movements as here supposed on the part of Russia, upon the two flanks, might politically affect the interests of other states in a manner to arouse decided and reasonable antagonism; for exerting which they have formidable facilities, by position and otherwise. These advantages, however, rest ultimately upon the sea, and consequently they will not, unless carefully improved, outweigh — or even equal — the predominance by land which Russia has, owing to her territorial nearness and other conditions already mentioned. Moreover, as contrasted with the political unity of Russia and her geographical continuity, the influences that can possibly be opposed to her are diverse and scattered. They find, however, a certain unifying motive in a common interest, of unfettered commerce and of transit in the regions in question. It is upon the realization of this interest, and upon the accurate appreciation of their power to protect it — and not upon artificial combinations — that correct policy or successful concert in the future must rest. Effective cooperation between nations depends upon the necessity imposed by a common interest; the more clear and general, therefore, the understanding of the interest and of attendant conditions, the more certain and abiding the co-operation.

The regions whose political and social future is in doubt, and to be determined possibly by the relative effect exerted upon their inhabitants by the contrasting powers of the land and of the sea, in the struggle of these to influence commercial conditions, constitute the objectives of policy. They are, on the east, the Chinese Empire, and more particularly China proper; on the west, Turkey in Asia and Persia. The latter two are conterminous, the line of division being marked by a lofty but not impracticable mountain chain, extending to the southeast from the ranges of Armenia nearly to the Persian Gulf. Being substantially devoid of railroads, this tract is commercially backward, judged by modern standards. Its area, omitting Arabia, is about a million square miles, distributed between two lines, roughly parallel, indicated on the south by the Mediterranean and the Persian Gulf, on the north by the Black and Caspian seas. The breadth thus bounded is about five hundred miles — one-half the distance from New York to Chicago. The interior is susceptible of great development, and, specifically, it offers opportunity for railroad communication from the Mediterranean to the head of the Persian Gulf, branching through Persia to the borders of India. From such a trunk line once in operation, lateral extensions would of course follow as improvements increase.

The question of dealing with countries such as these and China, in which governments and peoples alike are content to be stationary, neither knowing nor desiring progress, is so troublesome that it will be postponed until the day when the outside more advanced civilization has need of them; or until, as now with China, the future need is emphasized by a present consciousness of its imminence, and by a movement, more or less general, to obtain positions that can be utilized for control or influence. Whatever the nature of such influences, be they most contrary one to another, they have always this in common: they need some circumstance of advantage, in the possession of visible power and position, which alone the native occupants understand as a motive for concession. According as the relative impulses from the north and from the south compare in unmistakable force, so will they prevail. There can be, of course, no question of dispossessing the present inhabitants, that being neither practicable nor desirable. The rational object can only be to induce them to place themselves under such conditions as shall contribute to their regeneration, to their own benefit and that of the world at large. Whether this shall be effected by a gradual assumption of rule, as in India, or by actuating the government in nominal possession, as now in Egypt, is a matter of detail concerning which prediction is impossible. Results in such cases are matters less of formal preordainment than of growth — of evolution — stage by stage.

In the past the history of such changes has commonly been that private commercial enterprise leads the way, and that the incapacity of the local government permits the occurrence of abuses, which necessitate the interference of a foreign state to protect the rights of its citizens. Interference cannot be confined to mere remedy of the past and engagements for the future, but seeks prevention by guarantees, usually of such a description as to confer a certain degree of local rule. This, in turn, partaking of the vitality of its mother-country, tends to grow, as all life does. The seed, having been sown, germinates and thrives after its manner, which is not the manner of the soil; but, once planted, it is ineradicable. Whether it overspreads the land depends not upon the native resistance, but upon its meeting counteracting influence of a nature essentially akin to its own.

This process is in India a matter of past history, which had its crisis in the days when Clive and Dupleix represented the rival alien influences of Great Britain and of France; but it has received various illustrations in our own time. In Egypt its evolution is but lately complete, and there, as in India, quite contrary to what may have at first been expected, has resulted in the dominance of a single state. In China it has begun, and is still in progress. There it presents as yet only the competition of several nations; it remains to be seen whether, as has been the case in India and in Egypt, this condition will be radically modified by some sudden unanticipated event. That Asia Minor, Syria, Mesopotamia, and Persia will remain indefinitely strangers to experience of a like nature, is not to be imagined. There is no reason why they should, and there are very evident conditions which indicate that, although postponed, the first step is sure to be taken and the consequences sure to follow, although we cannot now foretell the time of the beginning nor the character of the issue.

Whatever the stage reached in a particular case, the general phenomenon has received sufficient demonstration to be accepted as a fact, in the light of which it becomes advisable to study the present, and to provide that the future should be less accidental than the past. This study can begin and rest upon the two generalizations already made: first, that the scenes of present movements are upon the two flanks of the same long line, the continuity of which is emphasized by the extension of Russian territory; and, second, that, from the obvious conditions, the struggle as arrayed will be between land power and sea power. The recognition that these two are the primary contestants does not ignore the circumstance that neither is a pure factor, but that each side will need and will avail itself, in degree, of the services of the other element; that is, the land power will try to reach the sea and to utilize it for its own ends, while the sea power must obtain support on land, through the motives it can bring to bear upon the inhabitants. To the second of these generalizations there is one conspicuous artificial exception. France, which on the immediate scene of interest is naturally a sea power, becomes by her formal and essentially subsidiary alliance with Russia an element of the land power in relation to the East. Other than that, the proclivities of the states concerned follow their natural interests — a condition which, by its greater healthfulness, promises a longer endurance. Hence ensues solidarity of interest between Germany, Great Britain, Japan, and the United States, which bids fair to be more than momentary, because the conditions seem to be relatively permanent.

Let us consider and state the conditions; for, taken together with those of Russia, they constitute the military, and therefore the political, situation on the flanks. Three of these states are preponderantly maritime, and in the matter of military force decisively naval. Germany is different; yet her commercial growth of late years places her necessarily on the side of those who wish commerce in these undeveloped regions to be unfettered. In common with the others, she must seek to provide against an exclusive control there, because she cannot expect such to fall to her. That she already seeks such provision is known, by the large additions proposed to her navy. We may assume, therefore, that in China, should necessity arise, the four states would be found following a common line of action, dependent upon naval force. Such force would find its bases near at hand, and yet, by simple naval predominance, adequately shielded from land attack — with the exception of Germany, which at Kiaochau is more vulnerable. Japan is protected by her strictly insular position, and Hong-kong by remoteness from the centres of possibly hostile land power. In the possession of the Philippines, the United States has — we may almost say forced upon her — a base similarly secure.

These conditions insure control of the sea to their navies, as now constituted. The power of the four states, if alive to the necessities of the case, outweighs in bases and in ships, in passive and in active force, in foundation and in superstructure, the naval possibilities of Russia and of France. But this pure sea power receives aid from land conditions. Upon one flank of the Russian line lies the army of Japan; upon the other, five thousand miles away, that of Germany. The latter consideration, by its bearing upon the problem of Asia, illustrates the direct interest of the United States in the continued vigor of a European nation. The two extremes of the Russian line, thus open to attack, are most inadequately connected by rail. The Philippines and Hong-kong lie similarly upon the eastern flank of the general position, separated from it only by water distances which are comparatively short and absolutely safe. To these supports, and to the facilities for action by land power, is to be added the long access for sea power into the interior afforded by the Yang-tse-kiang. Battle-ships can ascend as far as Nanking, 230 miles from the sea, and vessels of very considerable fighting power to Han-kow, 400 miles farther. Steamers of a kind much employed in the American civil war can go to Ichang, a thousand miles from the river's mouth.

A military situation is also a political condition, the right understanding of which conduces to peace. Advantages such as the above, coupled with a reasonable certainty that there is no purpose to use them for political aggression — however actively they may be employed for the offensive in case war unhappily arises — tend to prevent attempts to obtain commercial monopoly through military force. There is, however, one very weak element in the position of the sea powers, and that is the location of the Chinese capital. Because of the nature of their force, inadequate of itself to local territorial expansion, their aim must be to develop China through the Chinese, to invigorate and to inspire, rather than to supersede, the existing authority. It is to be wished, therefore, that the seat of government, despite the force of tradition, could be shifted to the Yang-tse-kiang, throwing itself frankly upon the river, as the core round which to develop a renewed China. Unless this be done, and in case the Peking authorities yield, as is the custom of Orientals, to the nearest strong pressure, it can hardly fail that a rival and opponent rule should gradually arise in the valley of the Yang-tse. The feebleness of the central government lends itself to such a revolution, which would be only a further development of the local independence already found. It may perhaps be for the welfare of humanity that the Chinese people and territory should undergo a period of political division, like that of Germany anterior to the

French Revolution, before achieving the race patriotism which, in our epoch, is tending to bind peoples into larger groups than the existing nationalities. The issue is one that passes human foreordainment; but the contemplation of the two alternatives is not amiss to the preparation of the statesman.

From our summary it seems evident that the four maritime states named can, by their positions on the eastern side of Asia, seriously impede advance from the north. On the western flank, embracing Persia and Asiatic Turkey, with the Levant Basin of the Mediterranean, conditions are less clear. The centre of the Russian strength is nearer, the sea power of France more at hand to support the Russian navy of the Black Sea — circumstances which favor a local predominance that for centuries has been, and still is, a leading ambition of France. As an offset, the engagements of Italy in the present state of international alliances, and her national sympathy, based upon evident interest, should prompt her active support to any combination the natural tendency of which shall be to insure the balance of power in the Mediterranean, and the consequent free use of the Suez Canal. The conspicuous political sagacity of her people cannot fail to realize that her geographical position, close to Malta and central as regards the Mediterranean Basin, enables her, by means of her powerful navy, to be a factor of decisive importance in this field, the most influential and yet most precarious link in the chain of European communications with the farther East. Neither immediate interest nor local circumstances of advantage justify either Japan or the United States in expending here any part of the energies they require for more pressing duties; and the people of the latter would certainly be loath, probably to the point of refusal, to help perpetuate the abused power of the Sultan — the more so because their traditional friendship for Russia can be alienated only by the latter promoting a policy distinctly hostile to their interests. Yet, while this is so, Americans must accept and familiarize their minds to the fact that, with their irrevocable entry into the world's polity, first by the assertion of the Monroe doctrine, and since by their insular acquisitions — above all, the Philippines — and by the interests at stake in China, they cannot divest themselves of concern, practical as well as speculative, in such a question as the balance of power in the Levant, or at the entrance of the Persian Gulf. In predominance in those quarters is involved, for the present at least, control of the shortest way from our Atlantic coast to our new possessions — that by way of the Red Sea; but still more is this road valuable to Great Britain and to Germany, whose policy in China is naturally in accord with, and therefore should be a support to our own. Consequently, what affects them in the one region necessarily affects us in the other.

The question of Persia and Asia Minor, regarded from the point of view of our study, concerns the safety of the shortest connection of our natural supporters with the point of interest common to us and to them. It is not their only route, and in so far its importance is lessened. Its value to them also suffers diminution, in the opinion of many, from the hazardous nature of the voyage in time of war, through the narrow waters of the Mediterranean, the yet more contracted Red Sea, and with the very vulnerable link between them, the Suez Canal. When to this is added the length of the Mediterranean — 2000 miles from Gibraltar to Suez — and the presence of the French navy, strongly based on the northern and southern coasts, it is not remarkable that a representative school of thought in Great Britain favors the frank relinquishment of so dangerous a course, and regards the canal simply as a convenience of peace. Yet while present political tenures continue, and still more if they are strengthened and developed on existing lines, it should be possible to reduce the perils of this transit, as expressed above, to a degree that would cast the balance in its favor, at least as an interior line for strictly military purposes, and against the greater security, but also much greater length, of the voyage around the Cape of Good Hope.

It is evident, however, that while such military security, if realized, depends primarily upon naval force, that force must rest for its foundation, its base, upon a reasonably secure territorial preponderance in the eastern Mediterranean, the great strategic centre of the route; upon a political condition there which shall assure, not a mere outpost like Gibraltar and Malta, but the support of an extensive population attached by ties of interest. The nucleus of such a combination already exists in the British occupation of Egypt, which, as before remarked concerning India, —

and the same is true of the Philippines, — not only confers an advantage, but entails an impulse to action. Be the insecurity of the canal route what it may, the work of Great Britain in Egypt carries an obligation to insure its continuance despite a state of war; and the effort necessary to secure Egypt will secure the canal, except against momentary closure by the premeditated sinking of a vessel. It is hardly to be supposed, however, that such a mishap cannot be avoided by a rigorous military control of vessels in transit, and of the pilotage, which will prevent sinking in mid-channel. Moreover, even if the canal be choked, the way remains far the shortest, in time, for military purposes, requiring only the transfer of troops or munitions of war across the narrow neck of land.

Under conditions of war, the continuance of Egypt in its present tenure, and the security of the shortest route to the East, both depend ultimately upon the permanent political bias of the region now called Turkey in Asia, and in a subsidiary degree upon that of Persia. That this is so will readily appear if we imagine that, instead of the existing misrule, Turkey in Asia — Asia Minor, Syria, and Mesopotamia — formed a highly developed modern state, with an efficiently organized army and navy. Nothing can be said now of the power of France in the western half of the Mediterranean that would not be as true, and truer, of the control of such a state over much greater issues. In its presence, if hostile, Egypt would be insecure, as she was in the days of the Ottoman vigor; and the strategic importance of Egypt's position is a commonplace of the ages. This imagined state, touching the Black Sea, the Persian Gulf, the Red Sea, and the Levant, would control the issues from vast territories to the outer world. It does not now exist; but the creation of such a political entity, and its development on healthy lines, are as much one of the problems of Asia, and as important, as China itself. The latter is primarily and chiefly a region simply of production; the other, while not barren in this aspect, would fulfil the far more vital rôle of controlling communications. In superiority of interest to the world at large, therefore, it far excels.

In order to constitute here a political condition susceptible of durable progress, in place of the present impotent misrule, a process of development must begin from without; for it is sufficiently demonstrated that there is no internal source of regeneration under the actual tenure. Whatever shall happen, the existing populations must remain; but the fate of the government, be that near or remote, will depend upon its faculty of accommodation to the dominant, though alien, pressure. During the stages of advance, through military organization and economical administration, both comformable to the genius of the outside force, be that Russian or Western, the fleet that there finds its territorial base of action will continue to be, not native, but that of the external power; for a navy is the most delicate, most specialized form of military institutions, and hence the latest to mature into independent life. Nevertheless, during the period of tutelage, the result upon the maritime strategic field will be the same as though the naval organization, as well as the military, were composed of the inhabitants themselves. Both embodying the genius of the educating power, the combination of the two will control in her interest this central position of the world.

It is clear, indeed, that here and in China, as well as in Egypt, and wherever a numerous population already exists, the regeneration precursory to full attainment of civilization must proceed through, and by, the inhabitants already in possession of the soil. Concerning this there can be, and should be, no dispute. It appears little less certain that these now have not, either in themselves or in their existing governments, the power to begin and to continue the necessary reformation. The question therefore is, under what impulse, under the genius of what race or of what institutions, is the movement to arise and to progress? The determination of the answer depends upon a struggle, peaceful or otherwise, between the external powers, — a conflict inevitable, irrepressible, because of their opposing political institutions, themselves the expression of the yet more vital force of contrasted national characters. Whatever the scene or the nature of the contest, whether it be decided upon the debatable ground itself or exterior to it, upon land or upon sea, by peaceful competition or by the arbitration of war, the issue depends upon a balance of force. That it is impossible of prediction is no reason for abandoning an attempt to appreciate the conditions. Quite the contrary; for, be the result what it may, there will enter into its determination not merely blind force, of numbers or of position, but intelligent direction as well, which shall be guided step by step, as emergency succeeds emergency, by informed understanding of the importance and character of the elements of the problem, and by a forecast — a long view — of the ends to be desired. This will be the more necessary on the part of the sea powers if they have the common interest that has been asserted; for, not being under a single head, community of action, without which they will be powerless, can proceed only from an accord based upon accurate comprehension of the issues at stake.

It must be observed that there is not in Levantine Turkey any free waterway, such as in China is given by the Yang-tse-kiang, opening a constant, ready access to the interior from the sea, although a certain analogy thereto is presented by the re-entrant angle formed by the coasts of Syria and Karamania, nigh to the apex of which lies the British island of Cyprus. The development of the interior, upon which alone is to be based that influence upon the inhabitants which shall bring them as a factor into the sphere of international relations, must be by land communications — by railroad — the main line of which, in the absence of watercourses navigable by large ships, will here form the core, around and from which the influences of civilization will grow. Failing immediate direct action by foreign governments, such development will fall to private enterprise, and will in its beginnings naturally follow the lines of least resistance and greatest advantage, which will be in the comparatively easy country that lies between and gives access to two seas — the Mediterranean and the Persian Gulf. Whatever the particular direction of such a road — which will depend chiefly upon local considerations — it must at once assume political, and therefore strategic, importance. This fact will probably induce a certain rivalry — based upon military as well as commercial reasons — to obtain the concession for building.

The recognition of a community of interest in the general question of Asia, as depending upon land and upon sea power, should influence those who possess the latter to guard sedulously against permitting this rivalry to degenerate into antagonism. This, if done, would illustrate conspicuously the healthful effect of broad general views upon immediate particular action. The nation that lays and administers such a road will, if politically discreet, affect the surrounding country by the daily evidences of benefit, conferred and to be expected; and thus, step by step, promoting organization and improvement, will secure that firm mass of territorial support which, when united to a sea power otherwise preponderant, will determine control. It is almost needless to say that the raw material of military power is in these regions abundant and good.

The considerations heretofore presented show the conditions and the possibilities upon the two extremities, or flanks, of that middle zone of Asia which is defined broadly by the thirtieth and fortieth parallels of north latitude. From them it may be inferred, concisely, that while the eastern regions — China and its dependencies — are of more immediate commercial concern to the rest of the world, and the decision of their future more imminent, those upon the west, finding their centre about the Levant and Suez, possess far greater military and ultimate importance, because they affect the question of communications between Europe, India, and China; not to speak of Australia, which also is therein interested, though less exclusively dependent. Unless Great Britain and Germany are prepared to have the Suez route to India and the Far East closed to them in time of war, they cannot afford to see the borders of the Levant and the Persian Gulf become the territorial base for the navy of a possible enemy, especially if it appear that the policy of the latter in the Pacific runs seriously counter to their own. From Gibraltar to India the Suez route is throughout comparatively narrow, and therefore stations which flank it — as Gibraltar, Algiers, Toulon, Malta, Aden, and the Persian Gulf — can more effectively exert control, because their comparative nearness cannot be overcome by a circuitous course. In the western basin of the Mediterranean such control, so far as dependent upon positions, irrespective of mobile force in ships — a most important qualification — is at present in the hands of France; but once past Sicily and Malta, the maritime situation changes with the geographical and political distribution. There is there no local dominant naval state, and the existence of such depends upon the political future of Asiatic Turkey and Persia.

It will be objected that for Great Britain and Germany to maintain their fleets in the Levant, dependent for re-enforcement and supply upon the home countries, is to occupy a position the communications of which, on account of the exposed stretch from Gibraltar to Malta, are unendurably defective, as the strength of a chain is that of its weakest link. The objection is perfectly sound, though not necessarily decisive even under present conditions, but it only makes clearer the need of a more solid territorial establishment in the Levant; one which, through the development of Asiatic Turkey, could afford a local self-sufficing base of naval operations. For, after all, nothing, not the sanding-up of the canal itself, can change the natural conditions which make Egypt the strategic centre of the chief highway between the East and West. It approached this even in the days of sailing-ships, as Nelson and Napoleon then recognized. Steam has made it so decisively; and before the canal was dug, travel had reverted to this route. In these days of big nations, Egypt, from its comparatively restricted habitable area, must remain the appendage of some greater state. Of which? Is it not apparent that the nearer at hand the stronger the tenure, because more susceptible of consolidation? As positions now are, British power territorially consolidated in the Levant, and with a preponderant fleet, can dominate the entire Mediterranean; for this, after all, is a small sea, which a superior fleet centrally placed can control to the full extent of security, as security is understood in war, and without difficulties exceeding those common to all military operations. Such a fleet would require simply to be able to receive harbor support at either end of the sea; for, while it must be able in case of urgency to go to either Gibraltar or Suez, with the certainty of finding needed supplies on the spot, it is not necessary to the protection of either that it be locally present. Nelson at Sicily and at Naples covered Sidney Smith before Acre and Alexandria. Granted a secure base of supplies in the Levant, Italy — too little considered in the question of the East — and Malta have the power, so far as position goes, to dominate the Mediterranean from east to west.

Not only is Great Britian for her own credit bound to hold Egypt, but the central position of the latter with reference to the whole Eastern world is such that, even under present drawbacks, it is hard to conceive any conditions in which supplies can fail to pour in from several quarters. In military situation, Egypt approaches an ideal;

for to a local concentration of force, defensive and offensive, operative in two directions, towards Gibraltar or towards India, it adds several streams of supply, so diverse in origin that no one navy can take position to intercept them all. Reduced to the fewest, they flow in by two channels, the Red Sea and the Mediterranean: how shall any one fleet close both? If the Mediterranean be blocked, the Red Sea remains, always the shortest route for India, Australia, and the Cape, to aid to the full extent of their resources, the sole essential being to provide that their resources be adequate. In the same case, Great Britain herself has the Cape route. If this be thought overlong, all the more reason not to abandon that of Suez antecedent to necessity arising. Does some temporary cause, disaster or other, make the fleet itself temporarily inferior? What retreat surer than that of passing the canal from the Mediterranean to the Red Sea, or the reverse? As for permanent naval inferiority, be it incurred at any time or any place, it means, of course, the collapse of British resistance.

In short, submitted to strict military analysis, it would appear that the proposition to abandon the Mediterranean and the Suez route, in favor of the Cape, is a strategic policy defensive rather than offensive, and proceeds from the assumption — probably not recognized — that in some way "war," to use Napoleon's jibe, "can be made without running risks." The truer solution for a state already holding Malta and Gibraltar would seem to be to grasp Egypt firmly, to consolidate local tenure there, and to establish in India, Australia, and the Cape sources of necessary supply, — whether manufactories or depots, — in ammunition and stores, against the chance of temporary interruption on the side of England. If this be true under conditions of isolation, it is yet more true at a period when the interests of both Italy and Germany coincide in general direction with those of Great Britain.

Whatever decisions may be reached as to practical expediency, based upon the limitations of a nation's power, the considerations that have been presented show convincingly the overmastering and permanent influence of the strategic centre in the Levant, due to the aggregation there of several features, each of which is of the first natural importance. It is difficult to resist the conclusion that these inalienable characteristics will ever invest the region, as a whole, with the significance which in successive past epochs emphasized the names of Alexandria and of Constantinople, as the concrete expression of great complex facts. To our own age the like meaning is conveyed more impressively by the word Suez; for in that little isthmus and its canal is concentrated for western Europe the question of access to the greater East. All the considerations that have been advanced as regards Asiatic Turkey, Persia, Egypt, the basin of the Mediterranean, etc., are in this connection but accessory, deriving their importance from the effect they may have upon the great line of communications whose most critical point is at the neck of land which joins Africa and Asia. Will it be the dictate, of prudence even, to forsake this line, for the long circumnavigation by the Cape of Good Hope? To pose the question with somewhat of brutal candor, is this shorter road possessed only by favor, subject to the will and power of foreign states? Is such a conclusion necessary, in view of evident rivalry of interests among other countries? And is it possible, without self-inflicted national humiliation, under the existing conditions, which are the results, the testimonials of a career that, step by step, has been increasingly to the lasting honor of Great Britain as a benefactor of mankind?

For some time to come, to the full reach of the farthest view opened by present indications, the world's general movement of assimilative progress will be, not north and south, but east and west; in both ways upon Asia, which now offers the greatest stimulant to all the tendencies that impel advance. The course and influence of these eastern and western movements will be modified and concentrated by the two isthmuses, Panama and Suez, where the shortest line compels the removal of natural obstacles by artificial means, which in the case of the latter have already been successful. Speaking broadly, the two canals will mark a line of division, south of which the efforts of commerce and of politics will be intrinsically much less important than those which occur to the north. Great, however, as will be the consequence of both canals, that of Suez must remain the greater; partly because there is not to it — nor in any near future can be — such an alternative as is presented by the transcontinental railroads of America; partly because there cluster about it natural conditions — the Strait of Gibraltar, the Black Sea and

Dardanelles, the Red Sea and the Strait of Bab-el-Mandeb, the political decadence of Turkey — that have no equivalent in the case of the American isthmus, and also international jealousies, to which the existing political distribution of the Western Hemisphere is less conducive.

If the generalizations of the last paragraph be correct, the question naturally arises, should they entail any modification in political habits of thought? Concerning this, if the assertions themselves, and the precedent statements upon which they rest, are accepted, it follows, first, that they become the primary consideration in the direction to be given to external policy; by which is not meant that all other considerations are excluded, but that, being secondary, they are to be viewed with strict reference to the first, as subordinate or contributory to it. This affects the importance of South Africa to Great Britain, in so far as effort there affects the necessary concentration upon the Isthmus of Suez. As regards the United States, the value of the Caribbean Sea, being the outworks of the Central American isthmus, is in every aspect largely inreased, and all indications of political change affecting it even remotely must be sedulously watched; but, on the American continent, south of the points whence influence can be effectually exerted upon the isthmus, the Monroe doctrine loses much of its primacy. If national honor demand, we can continue to assert it in its utmost present extension; but in view of the rapid pronounced transfer of the world's ambitions and opportunities to Asia, it is undeniable that the centre of interest has shifted afar, for us as for others. If the new stake be as large and as imminent as is believed, it is to be pondered whether we do not weaken our power for efficient action there by continuing pledged to the political — which is the military — protection of states that bear us no love. Concentration — exclusiveness of purpose — is the condition of successful action in national policy, as well as in military enterprise. Rightly understood, the southern extremities of the Eastern and Western hemispheres must for the time stand aside, as of subsidiary interest to the greater movements elsewhere occurring.

So far in our discussion attention has been fixed almost exclusively upon the peoples and the states external to Asia, or at least to the middle zone of so-called debatable ground, in apparent oversight of the teeming population of the latter. It has seemed, doubtless, as though these were being regarded as not even pawns in the game, but only as the stake to go to the stronger. Such, however, has not been the case. The condition of these peoples is not that of sheep to be owned, although in some respects it much resembles that of sheep without a shepherd; for strong and virile as may be their native characters in individual manifestation, much of the force of the Asiatic is expended in maintaining a dogged stationariness of development, which has settled at last into an apparent impotency for self-regeneration, whether of social institutions or of government. If this generalization be approximately correct — and there is much to justify it in the known conditions — it follows either that these races must remain thus immobile for an indeterminate future, — which is unthinkable, — or else that movement, progress, reform, must start from external impulses. In the latter case the question of the source and character of these impulses, in themselves, and in the changes that they would tend to beget in methods, and ultimately in character, organization, and action, is evidently of the first importance to the world. If the effective impulse should be mainly Slavonic, there will be a result of one character; if Teutonic, of another; if Asiatic, yet a different. Again, it will matter much whether races essentially homogeneous remain nationally one; or whether, from local distinctions now existing, they pass, at least for a time, into a condition of division into states politically independent and rivals. Far as the result lies beyond our present horizon, it is difficult to contemplate with equanimity such a vast mass as the four hundred millions of China concentrated into one effective political organization, equipped with modern appliances, and cooped within a territory already narrow for it. The character of the civilization which it is destined to receive, from the influences now surrounding and impinging upon it, will go far to determine the future of the world; for civilization, in final analysis, means, not material development in the external environment, but the elevation of personal, and, through personal, of national character.

It is not, therefore, in negligence of the future of these peoples, but in consequence of the immense importance to them, and to all, of the direction that future shall take, that the question of the character and relative strength of the external contestants for influence possesses such immediate interest. The variance of the latter — if such it be — is the opening chapter of a long history, the end of which is involved in no small degree in these its beginnings. It is a long, long view, and foresight unquestionably fails to see the end; but this far it can surely reach — that the elements of danger and of good are so certainly great that there must now be serious prevision, by careful measurement of conditions, sustained watchfulness, and vigorous effort, to insure that nothing unduly sudden or extreme occur — nothing revolutionary; that there shall be gained time, the great element of safety, by the operation of which transformation is retarded into evolution. For whatever the character of the process, the result cannot be to obliterate the qualities of these races, but to introduce them as factors into our existing civilization, from which they have for ages stood apart; in like manner as the Teutonic genius entered into the civilization of Rome, not by sudden convulsion — though with many a throe — but through a protracted process of development, under the reciprocal influence of race characteristics essentially as diverse, almost, as those of opposite sexes. That the result was thus happily protracted, to our own great gain at this present moment, was due, as Mommsen has indicated, to the foresight — the long view — of Cæsar; partial, doubtless, even in so great a man, partly, it may be, even unconscious, but seeing, nevertheless, unto conviction, from afar, the dangers that the conditions foretold, and turning his attention with the intuition of genius to the provision of a barrier, by advancing the borders and consolidating the outworks of the Roman state, until positions were held which should insure delay — the primary, though not the final, aim of all defensive dispositions.

Our first necessity, therefore, is to recognize that for European civilization in its turn has now arrived an important period, a day of visitation; that a process has begun which must end either in bringing the Eastern and Western civilizations face to face, as opponents who have nothing in common, or else in receiving the new elements, the Chinese especially, as factors which, however they may preserve their individuality — as is desirable, and as the Latin and the Teuton still do — have been profoundly affected by long-continued intimate contact, and in such wise assimilated that the further association may proceed quietly to work out peacefully its natural results. To effect this does not demand the merging of national characteristics, but it does require more than material development, even the indwelling of a common spirit, a gift far more slow of growth than the process of material advance. Thus as the Latin civilization at the moment of decisive confrontation with Teutonic vigor found its expression in the Roman law and the imperial idea, — of which the centralized Church was the natural inheritor, — our own, while embodying many diverse national types, finds its unity in the hallowing traditions of a common Christianity; which is not the unimproved inheritance of a single generation, a talent laid up in a napkin, but an ever-swelling volume of inbred spiritual convictions, transmitted habits of thought, which, by their growth from generation to generation, attest their unimpaired vitality.

Measured by this standard, the incorporation of this vast mass of beings, the fringe of which alone we have as yet touched, into our civilization, to the spirit of which they have hitherto been utter strangers, is one of the greatest problems that humanity has yet had to solve; but to us, having the light of past experience, there is concerning it no ground for doubt, much less for fear. The success with which, in our society of nations, the Latin and the Teuton types mingle, without losing their individuality or their respective spheres of manifestation and of influence, has been due mainly, if not exclusively, to that one spirit which during the critical period found its home in the hearts of each, and became the common possession of races so diverse and for so long estranged. In its sign, in truth, they conquered, for it broke down the wall of partition between them, as between the Jew and the Gentile, reconciling the antagonism of ages without impairing the permanence of type. We may be sure, therefore, that the difficulty now before us — of long estrangement, present lack of mutual comprehension, and ultimate unity to be attained — cannot be adequately regarded from the standpoint of mere commercial advantages — the short view of immediate interests. However such considerations may serve to further a policy suited to the wants of the distant future, it will be only as they are in a direction generally right, the determination of which must be otherwise estimated. All the factors already indicated in this paper, and such others as may hereafter appear in it or elsewhere, should be contemplated not only in the light of immediate advantage, but of that great inevitable future, when, aroused to the consciousness of power, and organized by the appropriation of European methods, these peoples, and especially China, shall be able to assert an influence proportionate to their mass, and to demand their shares in the general advantage. Those who live in that day will recognize then, what our duty to them requires us to realize now, how immense the importance to the world that their development has been not merely material, but spiritual; that time shall have been secured for them to absorb the ideals which in ourselves are the result of centuries of Christian increment.

For the gaining of this necessary time, we and our posterity have much to hope from the fact that our present world of civilization consists of strong opposing nationalities, and is not one huge, consolidated *imperium,* such as that of which Cæsar laid the foundation, driven thereto because the individual declension of the Roman citizen had destroyed the material from which the more healthful organism of earlier days could have been reconstituted. It is a weighty tribute to his genius, and to the wisdom of the more eminent among his successors, that by their adroit skill of adjustment an organization should have perpetuated its energy so long after vitality had departed from its frame. Fixed in this mould of arrested, or fulfilled, development, knowing only intestine turmoil, without recognized rival to stimulate it in the struggle for existence, and so to preserve it from stagnation and consequent decay, the great, centralized, unified world of that epoch resembled a building whose stability depends not upon solidity of foundation, but upon the equilibrium of a house of cards. The example may be commended to the study of those who, by increase of international organization, and consequent diminution of individual state action, would push to a similar fatal unification, under a centralized authority, our own world of civilization, already sufficiently bound in the traditions and customs which inevitably accumulate, like papers in pigeon-holes, about all continuous activities, political or individual. Contrast with this, and with the disorders into which Charlemagne's empire fell, after that unified organization was shattered by the lapse of centralized authority involved in his personal death, the energy of the broken warring communities that rolled back the Saracenic invasion and evolved the subsequent social order of Europe, but whose strength lay in the strenuous vitality fostered by constant competition among themselves. Nothing more fatal can be devised for the states of our civilization, and for that civilization itself, than the habit, happily not yet acquired, of looking for the solution of doubts and the adjustments of interests to a central external authority, the analogue of governmental fostering care for the private citizen — of "paternalism." The health of the community of states, as of the community of citizens, depends upon the vigor of the individual members, of which rational self-sufficingness is an inevitable attendant. The rivalries of national interests, and the sharp competitions thence arising, serve to perpetuate the strong contrasts of race temperament and political methods which now exist among us; and this virility of national characters, born and sustained in conflict, will on the one hand intensify the inner impulse communicated to the Asiatic, and on the other, by their very counteraction, will retard the day of formal exterior conformity, the premature arrival of which, complete in form but imperfect in spirit, is to be dreaded.

CHAPTER III

THE accentuating rivalry between the states of our civilization arising from the unstable conditions of China, long uneasily felt, but not formally avowed, is now approaching a moment resembling that fixed for the unveiling of a statue. The presence of the statue is no secret, the very folds of the drapery betray its outlines, yet it is as it were ignored, until the date fixed for display. From yesterday to to-morrow things continue essentially as they have been; yet we all know by experience how profound the change, the increased sense of imminence and of responsibility, when the curtain falls, and facts long dissembled are looked straight in the face. Without moving, we have traversed years of event. Action that seemed susceptible of indefinite procrastination appears now to have been too long deferred. Opportunities which might have been seized are seen to have passed irretrievably, because in heedlessness or indolence we noted not the day of visitation. But, as has been remarked, it is not China alone that lies within the debatable zone. With but slight modification of phrase, what has been said of her may be affirmed of Afghanistan, of Persia, and of Asiatic Turkey, on the other flank of the line.

In contemplating the possibilities of action, it must be repeated that consideration for the populations involved should have precedence of the interests of external nations — even of the one, or ones, taking action. This is not said as a cover or an apology for measures the originating motive of which may be national self-interest. Self-interest is not only a legitimate, but a fundamental, cause for national policy; one which needs no cloak of hypocrisy. As a principle it does not require justification in general statement, although the propriety of its application to a particular instance may call for demonstration. But as a matter of preparation, for dealing wisely and righteously with this great question, against the chance of occasion arising, — a mental preparation which no government can afford to postpone, — the very first element of a just and far-seeing decision must be the determination to bear in mind, and to give due precedence to, the natural rights and the future development of the peoples most directly affected. The phrase "natural rights" is chosen expressly to indicate those that result from the simple fact of being born; in this distinct from political or legal rights, which depend upon other fitnesses than that of merely being a man. Thus the claim of an indigenous population to retain indefinitely control of territory depends not upon a natural right, but upon political fitness, shown in the political work of governing, administering, and developing, in such manner as to insure the natural right of the world at large that resources should not be left idle, but be utilized for the general good. Failure to do this justifies, in principle, compulsion from outside; the position to be demonstrated, in the particular instance, is that the necessary time and the fitting opportunity have arrived.

The interests of the populations in these countries is by no means necessarily identical with those of the present governments, nor with the continuance of the latter in either form or person. These are not representative, in the sense that they either embody the wishes or promote the best welfare of the subject. They represent at most the incapacity of the people to govern themselves, and in their defects are the results of generations of evolution from a false system, unmodified by healthy opposition. Being what they are, should necessity demand their discontinuance, there need be no tenderness in dealing with them as institutions, whatever consideration may be shown to the incumbents of the moment.

It is, in fact, the inefficiency of the governments that chiefly gives rise to the present uneasiness. Were they otherwise, the balance of strength which now exists between the land and the sea powers, as already indicated, and the commercial interest of the latter in the preservation of peace, would naturally and easily determine their maintenance against any aggression that overpassed the fortunes common to all states, and threatened their permanence or independence. As it is, confronted with the imminent probability of a dissolution, neither the time nor the circumstances of which can be foreseen, the result of causes either internal or external, or both, other nations are compelled to seek the preservation of their own interests, by means which may employ the existing governments, if these are equal to the task, or may supersede them. That either alternative is repugnant to the genius and traditions of the United States, it is needless to say. Under the government of no party will she willingly initiate a process so contrary to her preferences, and the grave issues of which cannot be foreseen; but equally, under no government can she stand by and see substantial injury done to the welfare of her citizens by the undue preponderance of an inimical system of occupation or of influence.

Accepting the existence of the problem in the terms so far stated, a solution may be attempted. Granting outside interference at all, — which not only is most likely, but has actually begun, — the successful issue would be found in a condition of political equilibrium between the external powers, whereby the equality of opposing forces, resting each on stable foundations, should prevent the undue preponderance of any one state, or of any one force resulting from a combination of states, and which at the same time should promote, at the utmost rate consistent with healthy growth, the material and spiritual development of the populations affected. Thus would be hastened the desirable day when the latter, while still retaining their special traits and aptitudes, shall have been successfully grafted on to the civilization of Europe, which, whatever its shortcomings, certainly has produced the best fruits in the individual, social, and political well-being of its members. This vital change effected, these new branches will then be able to discharge all functions of self-dependent and self-governing peoples, such as now constitute the international commonwealth. Is it too much to say that in Japan, being a country of manageable dimensions, our own day has witnessed just such a change? — demonstrating the possibility of absorbing the benefits, intellectual as well as material, of a system hitherto alien, and of entering into the community of its life without sacrificing national individuality? And while it is doubtless true that Japan has not experienced the governmental paralysis of China, she has, since she felt the impulse of the foreigner, passed through a revolution of institutions, from which only recently she has emerged, to the general admiration, into the full enjoyment of all international dignity and privilege. It is evident, however, that the duration of such a process depends in some considerable degree upon the bulk of the subject by which it is undergone; and when this is large, as in China, the effect of external impulses will be accelerated in proportion to the number of points, or to the extent of surface, to which they are applied. Making every allowance for the adaptability of the people of Japan, to which so much of her success is to be attributed, it may plausibly be inferred that her comparative smallness of area and of population facilitated her progress; and that accordingly many points of contact will be favorable to the development of the greatly superior mass of China, by distributing the external influences among areas corresponding to those centres through which the respective powers may act.

To such diffusion of influences, and to assurance of equilibrium, the presence and differing interests of many states will tend. Nor will it be without benefit that the effects produced will represent very great differences of characteristics, corresponding to the national types engaged. In so great an aggregate as that of China, variety and contrast of result would be intrinsically good; and if they promoted political subdivision, that also probably would be beneficial, both for the internal administration of the country and for the general political equilibrium of the world. As has before been said, it is scarcely desirable that so vast a proportion of mankind as the Chinese constitute should be animated by but one spirit and moved as a single man. If not a diversity of governments, at the least a strong antagonism of parties, embodying opposite conceptions of national policy, is to be hoped, as conducive to the healthful balance of herself and of other countries. It was not wholly a mistake that some in the ancient world deprecated the ruin of Carthage, and the disappearance of her influence upon the international relations of the day, with the consequent fall of Rome into corruption within and excess without, through the abuse of power to which no adequate external check remained.

There is therefore no cause to lament the rivalries, nor the conflict of systems, represented by the various nationalities which are now impressing China with the consciousness of the urgency of their demands. The facts exist, beyond the chance of speedy reversal, and must now be accepted as they are: conditions of the immediate present, elements of the short view, by which current action must be modified. It is unpractical to expend emotion in regret for the inevitable; it is better utilized as a stimulus to action, preventive or remedial. The necessity now is to take the next steps as nearly as possible in the direction of the ultimate goal, the ascertainment of which has been the object of what has so far been said; in other words, to seek the speedy establishment of conditions under which there shall be a balance of influence between land power and sea power, and at the same time a minimum of friction between the two ensue. The problem, from its nature, especially demands study by the Teutonic nations, — Germany, Great Britain, and the United States; for to them, representing as they do one party to the case, co-operation — not alliance, nor even pledge — is necessary, and co-operation must depend upon identity of conviction, resting upon community of interest. A single state like Russia, equipped with a government embodying the simplest conception of political unity, escapes the embarrassment inevitable to several nations, of more complex organization, in which the wills of the citizens have to be brought, not to submission merely, but to accord; and that upon a matter not only of national policy, but of international understanding.

Of other countries, France, it may be presumed, is by her artificial connection engaged to some extent to the policy of Russia in the East; whether for better or for worse will depend upon the coincidence of this with her natural interests there. At present, the principal result of the alliance is to emphasize the divergence of interests internal to the group of Latin nations. This is probably inevitable, both as a historical consequence of their too great proximity, and from their present conflicting ambitions in the Mediterranean. Nor can there be left out of account here the sincerely cordial interest, both past and present, of the English-speaking nations in the progress and confirmation of Italian unity. This can scarcely fail to strengthen, by all the subtile force of sentiment, on the one side and the other, the bond of a common interest in the Mediterranean, which is created and unified by the historic and unceasing efforts of France for a preponderance there, intolerable to other states. In face of an immediate urgency like this, especially when supported by the might of Russia, it is unreal to appeal to an argument so phantasmal as a common Latinity; for France, after all, is Latin but imperfectly, in organization rather than in temperament. The Gallic admixture, whatever its advantages, apparently carries with it a lack of the steadfastness essential to the endurance of political combination. From these relations of antagonism follow two chief results: first, that the French positional control of the western Mediterranean is much weakened; and again, that there is no third racial genius comparable, in political influence, to the two by which the European pressure upon Asia is chiefly constituted,— the Slavonic and the Teutonic.

There remains to consider Japan, the importance of whose part is evident, because she is the one nation, Asiatic in genius as in position, which by efficiency of action, internal as well as external, has established and maintained its place as a fully equipped member of the commonwealth of states, under recognized international law. It has already been noted that the essential elements of her strength, being insular, place her inevitably in the ranks of the Sea Powers, and whatever ambitions of territorial acquisition upon the continent she may entertain must be limited in extent, because of the limited number of her own population compared to that of the mainland adjacent; farther than which, of course, it is not supposable that she can wish to extend her activities. Western Asia and the Mediterranean, for example, though inseparably a part of the broad world question which centres just now about China, are clearly beyond the scope of Japan. Like the United States, local conditions emphasize her primary interests in a particular region and in one continent. Unlike the United States, the contractedness of her area denies the expectation of a superfluity of force, disposable in remoter quarters; while the nearness, in Asia, of great rival powers diminishes still further the possibility of distant enterprises. Narrow restriction in local territorial occupancy, however, is common to all the interested states; except, perhaps, Russia. The others, on account of their distance, as Japan on account of her size, must expect to affect China by impulses imparted to the inhabitants through commercial and political relations, supported militarily by sea power, which, from its mobility, will be operative not only in the immediate locality, but wherever else throughout the world its force can be felt in checking an opposing influence — as, for instance, in the control of commerce to its own advantage and to the injury of an enemy.

In the kind and methods of their power, and in their immediate interests, the Teutonic group and Japan are at one; it is in the nature of the influence transmitted that they will differ, because the original genius and, still more important, the inherited traditions of the two are different. Japan has exhibited remarkable capacity and diligence in the appropriation and application of European ways; but these are to her as yet an external acquisition, a piece of property, not a part of herself. In the European peoples these same ways, as they now exist, are the exponents of national character, of habits of thought, the outcome of centuries of evolution, in which a transmitted civilization, once exterior, has undergone an assimilative process under the operation of distinctive national faculties and environment. Such a result carries with it the assurance of permanence; not, indeed, in the form of stationariness, but in nature and direction of movement. Japan, in fact, from our point of view, is still under the disadvantage, by no means irretrievable, that the exterior and material characteristics of European civilization have been received too recently and rapidly for entire assimilation. In the short time that has elapsed since national political conversion began, it is not possible that change can have penetrated far below the surface, modifying essential traits and modes of thought. This, indeed, can be effected healthfully only by the gradual processes of evolution.

In the matter before us, co-operation — not formal alliance — between Germany, Great Britain, and the United States would be a strictly natural condition, carrying with it a fair promise of continuance, because, being based upon a common interest, its exertion would be governed by ideas substantially the same in origin, in tradition, and in spirit. The accession of Japan as a partner, if it take place, as may be hoped, will be the expression of a political phase, more or less lasting; of an expediency, resting upon the fact that, land and sea power being for the time in opposition, her place is with the latter. But even so, and while acting together loyally for common ends, the subtle essential characteristics of race must make themselves felt, must impart a divergence of ideals and of influences, not by any means necessarily hostile. Japan, like China, is Asiatic; the appreciativeness and energy with which she has embraced European standards and ways are a favorable omen, giving perhaps the surest promise as yet in sight that these shall pass into the Asiatic life and remodel it, as the civilization of Rome passed into the Teutonic tribes. But the result in the latter case has been a Teutonic civilization, not a mere extension of that of Rome. So here, what we have to hope for is a renewed Asia, not another Europe; and to this end the willing acceptance — nay, initiative — of an Asiatic nation is perhaps the most potent factor.

It must, however, be recognized and candidly accepted that difference of race characteristics, original and acquired, entails corresponding temporary divergence of ideal and of action, with consequent liability to misunderstanding, or even collision. Such recognition is a necessary, as well as a most important, antecedent to provision for the future, in which we all hope for the prevalence of justice and peace. Divergence of interests generates contention, even among those of the same household; but where there exists a community of feeling and tradition to which appeal can be made, there is already a beginning of reconciliation, that is less easily found where misunderstanding results from divergence of temperament and ideals. Both sources of difficulty are present in our problem. The contrary interests and the positions of the land and the sea powers have been examined at some length. The differences of temperament that are now meeting in Asia have been more casually indicated, but they may be summed up in the three races, the Asiatic, the Slavonic, and the Teutonic, neither of which probably can yet give to the others the perfect comprehension expressed in the word "unanimity." It is a prime necessity to recognize these diversities, to appreciate them, and to accept them, as being not causes of complaint, but difficulties to be smoothed; not by abolishing them, which is impossible, but by allowing to each fair play, so long as it grows by its own inner energy, and does not attempt propagation by the alien means of armed compulsion. From such tolerant temper will ensue an adjustment corresponding to the true value of each element involved, which cannot be expected if essential differences are ignored, and the expectation of uniformity take the place of that of unanimity, confounding oneness of spirit with oneness of operation. The distant solution, which all three races should desire, for the common good of Europe and of Asia, is not the subversion of Asiatic genius or institutions, but the quiet introduction of the European leaven — which itself, even when long accepted, is modified in form by racial genius — and that this should be effected under conditions of mutual respect and kindliness, which will ensure its spread, if it possesses the advantages which we think.

It is again a paradox — but yet truth — to say that these conditions of equity and kindliness are only to be maintained by the presence of force; by just self-assertion, taking the shape of insistence upon equality of opportunity, and supporting its demand by such evident preparation of means as will compel due attention. Preparation — readiness — insures consideration; and consideration necessarily takes the form of courtesy, as well as imposes study and realization of conditions. Both tend to peace, by removing impediments to the full play and due effect of the many factors — position, numbers, race, temperament, political institutions, national aptitudes of every kind — by whose freedom to work their natural results, and to attain their natural levels, the adjustment of evolution, the only secure result, will be reached.

Consideration worthy of the name implies candid acceptance of all the factors, and patient effort to appreciate them; but while this is in one way a very complex process, because there are many details, it is simplified in conception by the recognition of a very few distinguishing features. There must be the speculative forecast of the distant future, hand in hand with the consciousness of what at the moment is possible; and there must also be embraced, in due relative proportions, the sense of primary duty to one's own country, and an unremitting regard to the real exigencies and needs of other peoples. For the latter, as well as the former, are part of the account; and states in their community, as well as citizens in their commonwealths, should be characterized by a public spirit which, while giving precedence properly to interests especially in their charge, is convinced also that these are best secured not by obstinately withstanding the progress of others, but by providing for its reasonable satisfaction.

In this spirit, then, let us give consideration to the demands of to-day, in the light of the long view of the distant future as so far set forth for acceptance. In the present backward political condition of Asia, which accurately reflects the want of political aptitude in its peoples, the lack of effective organization deprives her great mass of population of the power of effective initiative, limiting its present function to a load of inertia, of passive resistance to change, which is, indeed, no contemptible factor in the evolution of the future, but against which no immediate provision is necessary. In organized preparation for advance, Japan alone represents the Asiatic; and Japan, so long as in this respect by herself, is not big enough to contribute the weight upon which, as well as upon force of impulse, momentum depends. For the moment Japan is perforce confined to deciding which of the two other contending races is by character and ambitions most favorable, both to her immediate interests and to the free ultimate development of Asia in the line of its natural capacities; and upon these considerations she must shape her course.

Between the two other races, the Slav and the Teuton, there are well-recognized racial divergencies, which find concrete expression in differences, equally marked, of political institutions, of social progress, and of individual development. It is reasonable to believe that these differences are partly fundamental, deep-seated in the racial constitution, and partly the result of the environment amid which either has passed its centuries of growth. There is between them the antagonism that results from lack of mutual comprehension, while to that is added a conflict of interests, such as is inherent in their relative positions in Asia, as heretofore analyzed, and in their consequent necessary ambitions. To deal satisfactorily with such a condition it is first of all necessary to admit it; not to gloze truth with a thin and useless veneer of uncandid professions of good-will, diluted by mental reservations. That done, it may be profitably asked whether parallel lines may not run in one direction instead of in opposition; whether it may not be possible for us even to converge, accepting one another as we are, not exacting uniformity, but finding in the one object which attracts our aims a centre of unanimity rather than of discord. This, however, is impracticable unless each recognizes the crucial necessities of the other.

There can be little doubt that beyond substantial differences of racial characteristics, which find necessary expression in modes of action — for action is the materialization of spirit — the accidental line of separation between the two races, defining their interests and their ambitions, is denoted by the ideas of land power and sea power. This distinction proceeds alike from present possession and from present want. It inheres in their positions, both absolutely, and as related to the common objects of interest or of desire in Asia. It attaches conspicuously to the question of communications, of access to those objects. The Teuton, under the three great national heads, possesses the sea, from which the Slav is almost debarred. The Teuton is inferior in land power, for, in all his branches and settlements, he is geographically far removed from Asia, with which a great part of the Slavonic tenure is coterminous. The communications of Asia with the outer world are fullest by way of the sea; and here again it is the Teuton that leads, as well in naval as in commercial development, and by a superiority which admits no rival.

Essentially, this relative condition cannot be reversed; it can only be modified, and that to the extent of reasonable concession, not of equality. Its maintenance, being in the line of nature's dispositions, is a rule of healthy policy, that will dictate or control national demands for local influence or possession, as affecting preponderance upon the element with which the racial strength is identified. On the other hand, it must equally be recognized that each race absolutely requires some foothold, though an inferior one, on the field which is not primarily its own; and this common, reciprocal need indicates the quarters in which mutual concession must smooth the way towards adjustment.

For instance, it is abundantly clear that Russia can never be satisfied with the imperfect, and politically dependent, access to the sea afforded her by the Baltic and the Black Sea, under present conditions. It is to the writer equally clear that the European members of the Teutonic family, Germany and Great Britain, cannot possibly admit her predominance in the Levant — and through this over the Suez route — which would be acquired if the enclosed naval basin of the Black Sea were converted into an impregnable base, for exit and for entrance, by the acquisition of the Bosporus and the Dardanelles. There is not in the world a parallel to this combination of advantages for the secure development, drill, and egress at will, of a formidable fleet; while its situation relatively to the canal would revolutionize commercial conditions, in so far as dependent upon naval power. So strong is my conviction upon this point that, while heartily wishing the success of the British arms in the current war in South Africa, I should see compensation even for utter defeat and loss in the necessity for Great Britain then to concentrate upon the Mediterranean and the Levant, and, in accord with Germany, to preserve a predominance about the isthmus, including Asia Minor; thus assuring a route necessary to both nations, and for which that by the Cape of Good Hope is no adequate alternative.[1]

How and where, then, can concession be made to the sea wants of Russia? There are two quarters remaining, and only two; neither wholly satisfactory, and by that very fact confirming the essential isolation of the Slav from the sea. They will be repeated, with a brief mention of the advantages and disadvantages of each to the two parties chiefly concerned. There is the Persian Gulf, reached by land through Persia from the shores of the Caspian; and there is the seaboard of China, to which access is had through Siberia. The former involves an aggression upon Persia, or concession from her; for it can in no way be considered adequate to Russia's

---

[1] These words were written December 12, 1899.

ambitions unless it carries with it extensive and consecutive territorial possession, from her present southern limits in East Turkestan to the borders of the gulf. If this be obtained, Russia is placed upon the flank of India; she controls one issue of any possible railroad from the Mediterranean through the valley of Mesopotamia, and absolutely interposes between it and its prolongation to India. Besides this, although the Persian Gulf has no such absolute control of the route to the East, *viâ* Suez, as is conferred by predominance in the Levant, it nevertheless does afford a flanking position, and entails a perpetual menace in war. In addition, it may be remarked that the maintenance there, by Russia, of a navy sufficient to be a serious consideration to the fleets of Great Britain, and to those who would be her natural allies upon the sea in case of complications in the farther East, would involve an exhausting effort, and a naval abandonment of the Black Sea, or of the China Sea, or of both. Naval divisions distributed among the three could not possibly give mutual support. Such a situation, contrasted with the secure, though long, access to the China sea coast, through territory either her own or under facile control, and with a fleet concentrated there, on the spot of greatest interest to the world, presents drawbacks so obvious that there is no motive, in the good of Russia, for the other states to consent to an arrangement which carries with it hazard to them. On the other hand, it appears unreasonable, and needlessly provocative of bad feeling, to object to her reaching the sea on the seaboard of China. Thus, here again, by an inevitable operation of a line of least resistance, we find on the eastern flank of the debatable zone, as on the western, the clustering of the nationalities, the gathering of the eagles, around a central interest, which derives its disputable character from the moribund condition of the local government.

In acknowledgment of their willing acquiescence in this coast tenure, opening free communication into the seas of the world, the sea powers may reasonably claim equal candor of admission that the navigable stream of the Yang-tse-kiang is their necessary line of access into the land, and the nucleus essential to the local spread of their influence. Like all arrangements here suggested, this reciprocal agreement should not be in the nature of formal convention, but of an understanding; which is not arbitrary, but rests upon existing facts that receive recognition in a spirit of mutual concession. It carries the corollary that there shall not be established upon the banks of the Yang-tse-kiang, by fortification or otherwise, any military tenure by which its waters can be forcibly closed to the sea powers. That the latter, under such conditions, will refrain during peace from using their own naval strength to debar others from commercial use of the river is insured; partly by the settled policy of the one among them that now has the greatly preponderant navy, partly by the mutual watchfulness between themselves which is inseparable from all combinations of states. In this instance co-operation among the naval nations depends upon a common opposition to a particular movement, naturally antagonistic to them, and upon a common interest, which, being accurately understood, will prevent measures that inure to the disproportionate sway of any one of them.

In fact, as regards possible aggression upon China, land power, being the prerogative of a single state, near at hand, is far more to be feared than sea power; for the latter is distributed among several, the bases of whose national strength are remote, and moreover it is in its methods more promotive of benefit, for it finds the sources of its vigor in commerce — only secondarily in force. It is therefore especially interested in elevating, rather than in subjugating, those with whom it deals, and the aim here, for the welfare of the world, should not be compulsion, but influence; not the appropriation of these countries, by one or by many, but the gradual evolution of their inhabitants, through material progress, and through mental contact with a civilization that has so far given the highest individual and social results. That such a process should be underlain by force — force of intrusion on the part of the outside influences, force of opposition among the latter themselves — may be regrettable, but it is only a repetition of all history. Force has been the instrument by which ideas have lifted the European world to the plane on which it now is, and it still supports our political systems, national and international, as well as our social organization.

In summary, therefore, and with respect both to the remote future and to immediate policy, the issue of events in the seas of China and in the Levant, in the extreme east and extreme west of Asia, will depend upon the presence of force, evident in positions occupied and in numbers available. This condition, at once natural and inevitable, dictates co-operation — not formal, but none the less clearly conscious — between the Teutonic nations, because of their fundamental identity of interest, which is the material factor, and because the conduct to which that interest and the nature of their power alike impel is animated by one spirit. That is the spirit of commerce — of interchange — essentially free, and desirous of an influence which, although it can and must be maintained by naval force locally displayed, cannot be widely diffused by the same agency; because the conditions of its strength narrowly limit its extension inland, making it for this chiefly dependent upon native local support. For effects, present and future, the sea powers must rely upon evident benefit following from association with them; a means which induces acceptance, not submission. Their force, resting on the sea, can serve only to frustrate attempts to exclude themselves, or, if occasion arise, to aid the populations concerned in resistance to subjection. To accomplish these things they must work together; not in the letter of alliance, which fetters, but in the spirit of accord, which comprehends.

From existing elements of opposition, the future of Asia will remain a question in which military considerations must predominate; until, at least, antagonism shall have passed into adjustment. Thus regarded, the nature and direction of effective co-operation are indicated by the geographical conditions which constitute the strategic situation. These have been discussed at large in the previous papers. It is enough to recall here, in summary, that the chief centre of interest, because of its extent and present unsettled state, is China, around which, however, are grouped the other wealthy districts, continental and insular, which constitute eastern Asia, from Java to Japan. These markets of the future are the near objectives of the political and military discussions which now attract attention; but beyond them, in any statesmanlike view, lies the remote future result upon Asiatics of the impressions they may receive in absorbing and assimilating European civilization. Will they, from the effects thus wrought upon them, enter its community, spiritually, as equals, as inferiors, or as superiors? politically, as absorbing, or absorbed?

Except Russia and Japan, the several nations

actively concerned in this great problem rest, for home bases, upon remote countries. We find therefore two classes of powers: those whose communication is by land, and those who depend upon the sea. The sea lines are the most numerous and easy, and they will probably be determinative of the courses of trade. Among them there are two the advantages of which excel all others — for Europe by Suez, from America by way of the Pacific Ocean. The latter will doubtless receive further modification by an isthmian canal, extending the use of the route to the Atlantic seaboard of America, North and South.

Communications dominate war; broadly considered, they are the most important single element in strategy, political or military. In its control over them has lain the pre-eminence of sea power — as an influence upon the history of the past; and in this it will continue, for the attribute is inseparable from its existence. This is evident because, for reasons previously explained, transit in large quantities and for great distances is decisively more easy and copious by water than by land. The sea, therefore, is the great medium of communications — of commerce. The very sound, "commerce," brings with it a suggestion of the sea, for it is maritime commerce that has in all ages been most fruitful of wealth; and wealth is but the concrete expression of a nation's energy of life, material and mental. The power, therefore, to insure these communications to one's self, and to interrupt them for an adversary, affects the very root of a nation's vigor, as in military operations it does the existence of an army, or as the free access to rain and sun — communication from without — does the life of a plant. This is the prerogative of the sea powers; and this chiefly — if not, indeed, this alone — they have to set off against the disadvantage of position and of numbers under which, with reference to land power, they labor in Asia. It is enough. Pressure afar off — diversion — is adequate to relieve that near at hand, as Napoleon expected to conquer Pondicherry on the banks of the Vistula. But if the sea powers embrace the proposition that has found favor in America, and, by the concession of immunity to an enemy's commerce in time of war, surrender their control of maritime communications, they will have abdicated the sceptre of the sea, for they will have abandoned one chief means by which pressure in one quarter — the sea — balances pressure in a remote and otherwise inaccessible quarter. Never was moment for such abandonment less propitious than the present, when the determination of influence in Asia is at stake.

Of the three Teutonic nations — Germany, Great Britain, and the United States — the two former alone are immediately interested in the Levant; because, independent of its local resources, the most vulnerable part of their necessary communication with the East is there. For its protection they have ample naval strength, if to the latter adequate local support is given. For this there is a nucleus in the central positions of Egypt and Cyprus, flanked as these are by Aden on the one side, by Malta and Gibraltar on the other; but there is further needed, unquestionably, in the region defined by the Black Sea and the Mediterranean, the Caspian and the Persian Gulf, that predominance of political influence which rests upon consciousness of interest implanted in the inhabitants; upon their dependence for security against a dreaded aggression; and upon their sense of benefit, anticipated for the future as well as bestowed in the past and present.

Preponderance such as this is conferred by

commercial enterprises for the development of a country, provided the nation by which they are undertaken supports them by its power, expressed by its wealth, and, in case of necessity, by its organized military forces. This is the necessary aim of the states which find in the Suez Canal their shortest route to the farther East. It is more particularly that of Great Britain, because she has extensive responsibilities in India, which may at any time require the use of that shortest route, not for commerce merely, but for troops. For the latter purpose, even the blocking of the canal, necessitating transshipment of troops and goods, would only lessen, not destroy, the gain in time over the Cape voyage. Germany's interest, while differing in kind and in degree, is no less real; and the irreversible fact remains that in the entrance of the Black Sea, in the valley of Mesopotamia, and in the table-lands of Asia Minor, by virtue of their natural features, of their extent, and of their central position, rests an ultimate control of the eastern Mediterranean, resembling that exercised some centuries ago by the Ottoman Turks. In the days of sails, however, loss of control did not involve exclusion from the best sea road to the

East, as it now would. The matter is preeminently the concern of Germany and Great Britain; but with theirs is associated that of Italy, because France has deliberately cast in her lot with Russia, which, by the nature of things, must be opposed alike to Latin and Teutonic predominance in the regions named. It lies beyond the scope of United States' activities, but not outside of our lively solicitude. It affects us in that it touches to the quick the freedom and rapidity of intercourse with the East on the part of those whose policy there must run even with ours, because of the similarity which characterizes alike our strength and our interests.

To state such a fact as this, with the reasons supporting it, is simply to indicate what has been before called the long view, the distant goal, which, to borrow a simile from the sea, may be steered for direct when the wind of circumstances is fair; but with the many complications that exist, or that may arise, each generation of statesmen must contend as the seaman of a few years back contended with contrary winds or currents. But, while so doing, they will not be helped, but hindered, if amid present difficulties they lose sight of ultimate aims; as if, to continue our parallel, the seaman forgot his destination in his attention to the wind. Neither in politics nor in seamanship can the course at any moment set disregard the port desired, nor in either profession does neglect of charted data conduce to success.

The people of the United States and their successive governments have not now, nor are likely to have hereafter, in connection with the future of Asia, to consider any such complicated conditions as are presented by the surroundings of the Suez Canal and of the Levant. Our difficulty at present does not proceed from outside conditions, but from those internal to our own national habits of thought, which in the past have been distinctly averse to studying external political problems, and even to admitting their existence, until pressed home upon our consciousness by an immediate emergency. Startling as has been the effect produced upon public sentiment by the recent exigency which threw the Philippines upon our hands, it must be remembered that a mental temperament evolved and ingrained by generations of acceptance, not merely inert, but willing, must tend to revert, as passing time dulls the sharp impression and lively emotions that followed the war with Spain. Most persons have experienced that, in forming or in breaking habits, the first few days under the impulse of a recent resolve are comparatively easy, but that to them succeeds an uninteresting monotonous period of struggle, which too often issues in apathetic surrender to former conditions. With nations the tendency is the same. To resist it, where resistance is necessary, there is required a comprehension of facts, and a recognition of the duties and interests involved; for in these, distant or immediate, are to be found the only unanswerable reasons and durable motives for national policy.

The argument of these papers rests upon the assumption, now quite generally accepted, that in the wide movement of expansion which has characterized the last quarter of the closing century, the Pacific Ocean in general and eastern Asia in particular are indicated as the predominant objects of interest, common to all nations, both in the near and in the remote future. Within the home dominions of the European and the American powers no marked territorial changes are to be expected; but in the outer world, where conditions are unsettled, and towards which all eyes are turned, regions even extensive derive their present significance less from their intrinsic value than from their bearing upon access to the central objects named. South Africa, for instance, if Mr. Bryce's estimate is correct, receives from its great gold-fields but a temporary importance, destined soon to disappear by their exhaustion; but as an important outpost on one of the highroads to India and the farther East it has some permanent value, which may be more or less, but in any event demands consideration.

The Isthmus of Suez, the Levant, and Persia in like manner possess inherent advantages; but it has been attempted to show that the enjoyment of these is a less pressing concern than the establishment there of political conditions which may affect the future control of the Suez route.

These, and the other factors named, by their particular values and their mutual influence, constitute the strategic features of the general world situation involved in the problem of Asia. With them nations have to deal in the light of their individual interests, checked by due respect to the rights of others, measuring the latter not exclusively by the rule of conventional ideas, essentially transitory, but by the standards of eternal justice, which human law can express only imperfectly. Nor does the mighty power of sentiment fail to find due place in such a scheme; on the contrary, when healthy in character, it receives from the considerations that have been adduced the intelligent direction which alone makes it operative for good. But a very large part of a nation's wisdom consists in reinforcing its own strength by co-operation with others, based upon a substantial identity of interests; and if such identity is found combined with community of character and tradition, fostering community of ideals, the prospect of continued and harmonious co-operation is greatly increased. From the sense of such kinship springs a sound affection, which redeems interest from much of the selfishness associated with the word. Such is the triple bond which may unite Germany, Great Britain, and the United States; not in alliance, but in solidarity of action, founded upon the rock of common interest, and cemented by the ties of blood.

In eastern Asia and the Pacific, although the interests of the United States are not identical with those of Germany and of Great Britain, they are alike; not the same, but similar. Rightly understood, while the three nations will be competitors, — seekers of the same end, — they should not be antagonists. For this reason our sympathy should go with the others in whatsoever, by facilitating their influence, tends towards the furtherance of the common policy. This needs especially to be understood in matters affecting the communications with the East; for there, the effect being indirect, and exercised in quarters remote from our own activities, understanding and sympathy are less easily aroused, and greater attention is required to comprehend. That upon such instructed appreciation of facts, when fully assimilated, there should follow a certain mutual regard, will be natural. Like will to like.

In return we may claim, and will doubtless receive, the same intelligent recognition and sympathy that we ourselves extend. Upon no other condition than a clear perception, where the respective paths and duties lie apart, can we reach that accord which will enable us to act in concert where they coincide. Of the two great lines of communication — Suez and Panama — the former, as a matter of political action, is wholly theirs; the latter, necessarily ours. If it should ever happen that either group come to the help of the other on its own ground, either by active interference or by unmistakable moral support, — as Great Britain is reported to have withstood foreign combination against us at the opening of the Spanish war, — it must not be with any idea of subsequent claim to local political interference. We work together when mutual interest requires, but in accordance with well-understood conditions; beyond that we stand clear of each other's business, knowing that misplaced meddling separates closest friends.

The writer has too often already discussed, directly or incidentally, the strategic situation which finds its centre in Panama to repeat the same here; but one or two remarks about Monroe doctrine may be not out of place. Accepting as probably durable the new conditions, which have so largely modified the nation's external policy in the direction of expansion, there is in them nothing to diminish, but rather to intensify, the purpose that there shall be no intrusion of the European political system upon territory whence military effect upon the Isthmus of Panama can be readily exerted. For instance, should a change anticipated by some occur, and

Holland enter the German Empire, it will be advantageous that it should even now be understood, as it then would be necessary for us to say, that our consent could not be given to Curaçao forming part of that incorporation. The Isthmus of Panama — in addition to its special importance to us as a link between our Pacific and Atlantic coasts — sums up in itself that one of the two great lines of communication between the Atlantic and the farther East which especially concerns us, and we can no more consent to such a transfer of a fortress in the Caribbean, than we would ourselves have thought of acquiring Port Mahon, in the Mediterranean, as a result of our successful war with Spain.

Consideration of interests such as these must be dispassionate upon the one side and upon the other; and a perfectly candid reception must be accorded to the views and the necessities of those with whom we thus deal. During the process of deliberation not merely must preconceptions be discarded, but sentiment itself should be laid aside, to resume its sway only after unbiassed judgment has done its work. The present question of Asia, the evolution of which has taken days rather than years, may entail among its results no change in old maxims, but it nevertheless calls for a review of them in the light of present facts. If from this no difference of attitude results, the confirmed resolve of sober second thought will in itself alone be a national gain. This new Eastern question has greatly affected the importance of communications, enhancing that of the shorter routes, reversing political and military — as distinguished from mercantile — conditions, and bringing again into the foreground of interest the Mediterranean, thus reinvested with its ancient pre-eminence. For the same reason the Caribbean Sea, because of its effect upon the Isthmus of Panama, attains a position it has never before held, emphasizing the application to it of the Monroe doctrine. The Pacific has advanced manifold in consequence to the United States, not only as an opening market, but as a means of transit, and also because our new possessions there, by giving increased opportunities, entail correspondingly heavier burdens of national responsibility. The isthmian canals, present and to come, — Suez and Panama, — summarize and locally accentuate the essential character of these changes, of which they are at once an exponent and a factor. It will be no light matter that man shall have shifted the Strait of Magellan to the Isthmus of Panama, and the Cape of Good Hope to the head of the Mediterranean.

The correlative of these new conditions is the comparative isolation, and the dwindled consequence, of the southern extremes of Africa and America, which now lie far apart from the changed direction imposed upon the world's policies. The regions there situated will have small effect upon the great lines of travel, and must derive such importance as may remain to them from their intrinsic productive value. Does there, then, remain sound reason of national interest for pressing the Monroe doctrine to the extent of guaranteeing our support to American states which love us not, and whose geographical position, south of the valley of the Amazon, lies outside of effective influence upon the American isthmus? Does the disposition to do so arise from sound policy, or from sentiment, or from mere habit? And, if from either, do the facts justify retaining a burden of responsibility which may embarrass our effective action in fields of greater national consequence — just as South Africa may prove a drain upon Great Britain's necessary force about Suez?[1] In short, while the principles upon which the Monroe doctrine reposes are not only unimpaired, but fortified, by recent changes, is it not possible that the application of them may require modification, intensifying their force in one quarter, diminishing it in another?

Not the least striking and important of the conditions brought about by the two contemporary events — the downfall of the Spanish colonial empire and the precipitation of the crisis in eastern Asia — has been the drawing closer together of the two great English-speaking nationalities. Despite recalcitrant objections here and there by unwilling elements on both sides, the fact remains concrete and apparent, endued with essential life, and consequent inevitable growth, by virtue of a clearly recognized community of interest, present and future. It is no mere sentimental phase, though sentiment, long quietly growing, had sufficiently matured to contribute its powerful

[1] Since these words were written the troubles in China, and the necessity of Great Britain to draw troops from India for service there, have enforced this particular illustration of the military embarrassments that may attend widely extended political responsibility. It is clearly the part of wisdom to retrench these where it can honorably be done, limiting minor activities, and concentrating purpose upon the necessary and greater external interests of the nation.

influence at the opportune moment; but here, as ever, there was first the material, — identity of interest, — and not till afterwards the spiritual, — reciprocity of feeling, — aroused to mutual recognition by the causes and motives of the Spanish war. That war, and the occurrences attendant, proclaimed emphatically that the two countries, in their ideals of duty to the suffering and oppressed, stood together, indeed, but in comparative isolation from the sympathies of the rest of the world.

The significance of this fact has been accentuated by the precision with which in the United States the preponderance of intelligence has discerned, and amid many superficially confusing details has kept in mind, as the reasonable guide to its sympathies, that the war in the Transvaal is simply a belated revival of the issue on which our own Revolution was fought, viz., that when representation is denied, taxation is violent oppression. The principle is common to Great Britain and to us, woven into the web of all her history, despite the momentary aberration which led to our revolt. The twofold incident — the two wars and the sympathies aroused, because in both each nation recognized community of principle and of ideals — indicates another great approximation to the unity of mankind; which will arrive in due time, but which is not to be hurried by force or by the impatience of dreamers. The outcome of the civil war in the United States, the unification of Italy, the new German Empire, the growing strength of the idea of Imperial Federation in Great Britain, all illustrate the tendency of humanity to aggregate into greater groups, which in the instances cited have resulted in political combination more or less formal and clearly defined. To the impulse and establishment of each of these steps in advance, war has played a principal part. War it was which preserved our Union. War it was which completed the political unity of Italy, and brought the Germans into that accord of sentiment and of recognized interest upon which rest the foundations and the continuance of their empire. War it is which has but now quickened the spirit of sympathy between Great Britain and her colonies, and given to Imperial Federation an acceleration into concrete action which could not otherwise have been imparted; and it needed the stress of war, the threat of outside interference with a sister nation in its mission of benevolence, to quicken into positive action the sympathy of Great Britain with the United States, and to dispose the latter to welcome gladly and to return cordially the invaluable support thus offered.

War is assuredly a very great evil; not the greatest, but among the greatest which afflict humanity. Yet let it be recognized at this moment, when the word Arbitration has hold of popular imagination, more perhaps by the melody of its associations, — like the " Mesopotamia" of the preacher, — than by virtue of a reasonable consideration of both sides of the question, of which it represents only one, that within two years two wars have arisen, the righteous object of either of which has been unattainable by milder methods. When the United States went to war with Spain, four hundred thousand of the latter's colonial subjects had lost their lives by the slow misery of starvation, inflicted by a measure — Reconcentration — which was intended, but had proved inadequate, to suppress an insurrection incited by centuries of oppression and by repeated broken pledges. The justification of that war rests upon our right to interfere on grounds of simple humanity, and upon the demonstrated inability of Spain to rule her distant colonies by methods unharmful to the governed. It was impossible to accept renewed promises, not necessarily through distrust of their honesty, but because political incapacity to give just and good administration had been proved by repeated failures.

The justification of Great Britain's war with the Transvaal rests upon a like right of interference — to relieve oppression — and upon the broad general principle for which our colonial ancestors fought the mother-country over a century ago, that "taxation without representation is tyranny." Great Britain, indeed, did not demand the franchise for her misgoverned subjects, domiciled abroad; she only suggested it as a means whereby they might, in return for producing nine-tenths of the revenue, obtain fair treatment from the state which was denying it to them. But be it remembered, not only that a cardinal principle upon which English and American liberty rests was being violated, but that at the time when the foreigners were encouraged to enter the Transvaal franchise was attainable by law in five years, while before the five years had expired the law was changed, and the privilege withdrawn by *ex post facto* act.

In each of these wars one of the two nations

which speak the English tongue has taken a part, and in each the one engaged has had outspoken sympathy from the other, and from the other alone. The fact has been less evident in the Transvaal war, partly because the issue has been less clear, or less clearly put, chiefly because many foreign-born citizens of the United States still carry with them the prepossessions of their birthplace, rather than those which should arise from perception of their country's interest.

Nevertheless, the foundations stand sure. We have begun to know each other, in community of interest and of traditions, in ideals of equality and of law. As the realization of this spreads, the two states, in their various communities, will more and more closely draw together in the unity of spirit, and all the surer that they eschew the bondage of the letter of alliance. To complete the group, ethnically and spiritually, there is needed the accession of the other branches of the Teutonic family, of which the German Empire is the great exponent. The race can afford to wait for this, and it would certainly be injudicious to precipitate its coming by a forcing process; still, it may be remarked that the period of incipiency, in which the Anglo-American concord of tendency still remains, is the most favorable moment for the entrance of a third party, akin to the other two.

In conclusion a further remark may be offered. Both the signs of the times and obvious motives for action point to a probable permanent co-operation between the communities which speak the English tongue, as well as to a possible, if much less assured, coincidence of action with the empire the language and people of which come from the same stock, though differentiated by prolonged separation. But upon the horizon of the future may be descried a further omen of favorable augury. Various causes have conspired during the passing century to depress the visible power and influence of the Latin communities in Europe, compared to those grouped as the Teutonic. The unification of Italy is the one conspicuous exception. To this let there be added the strategic central position of the new state in the Mediterranean, which is to Europe far more even than the Caribbean can be to America, and also the political considerations which have forced her and France into the opposite scales of the political balance.

This attitude of Italy cannot but be fully confirmed by the clear necessity, to Latin and to

Teuton, to insure that predominance in the Levant which is essential to both, because, as sea powers, secure use of the Suez Canal is to them vital. The significance of this is that, by the force of circumstances, Italy, the modern representative of that which is most solid, politically, in the original Latin strain, remains in the intimacy of political attachment with the Teutonic Powers. This assures us the continued association of that Latin element which has contributed so much to the composite result of our Christian civilization; and it still more points on to the time when that element, the lineal inheritor of Roman greatness, seeing more clearly where its interests lie, shall find in Italy the centre and the pattern which shall restore it, in renewed glory, to the commonwealth of states that already owes to it so much.

NOTE — Since concluding these papers the writer has met these recent words of Sir W. W. Hunter (introduction to *History of British India*), whose regretted death has just removed one of the most widely informed students of Asian questions : " I hail the advent of the United States in the East, as a new power for good, not alone for the island races that come under their care, but also in that great settlement of European spheres of influence in Asia, which, if we could see aright, forms a *world problem* of our day."

THE EFFECT OF ASIATIC CONDITIONS UPON WORLD POLICIES

SINCE the latest of the preceding papers was penned, the speculative forecast of the long view in political matters, whether pertaining to the nation or to the world, characterized as it inevitably has to be by general and contingent estimates, has perforce given place for the moment to that narrower but far more vivid realization of present transient conditions which is imposed by an immediate necessity. A common risk of an immense calamity, and a common insult received, have forced upon the nations of European civilization the recognition of their solidarity of interest as towards Asia, in so far, that is, as she adheres to her immemorial conservatism, antagonistic to the standards of conduct which we have reached, through an age-long progress that is still in continuance.

In the European family are evidently to be included the people of the United States, as direct inheritors therefrom by blood and by accepted tradition, and also, more significantly still, Japan, if her claim be admitted, as I think it should be. Her accession is indeed the more creditable to her national genius, because she enters the group in the more difficult and more self-determinative character of a convinced, and therefore willing, convert; not ignoring, nor depreciating, her own racial distinctiveness and historic past, but having the wisdom to see and to associate to herself the advantages in a system, not only of practice, but of thought as well, foreign to her previous habits. If nothing more than the mere adoption of obvious material improvements constituted the development of Japan, little but apprehension could be excited by the aptitudes she has displayed; but in that she shows herself open as well to influence by the ideals, intellectual and moral, which by gradual evolution have possessed us, there is the better hope. It is well worthy of consideration whether we may not see in Japan the prepared soil, whence the grain of mustard seed, having taken root, may spring up and grow to the great tree, the view of which may move the continental communities of Asia to seek the same regenerating force for their own renewal.

In this conversion, Japan is repeating the experience of our Teutonic ancestors, as they came into contact with the Roman polity and the Christian Church; with the advantage to her and to us that it may reasonably be claimed for our present civilization that it is not now in the condition of incipient political, and advanced moral, decadence which Rome had then reached, and which the Christian leaven, though it had begun to permeate, had not been able sensibly to retard. It is well for us, and for Japan as an influence in Asia, that the vitality and virility of the European states, including America, are not on the decrease, but on the increase, for good and not for evil. Her own participation in the spirit of the institutions of Christendom, as distinguished from its exterior manifestations in material results, is yet too recent to permit of maturity, — of strength to stand alone. She needs still the support and encouragement given by the example of great visible success wrought by a quickening spirit, of which the secret lies beneath the surface, which can be learned and understood by effort, but can be appropriated, made one's own, only by the discipline of long practice and the transforming power of a new ideal. To such discipline and influence Japan must be content to submit herself — not as to a yoke externally imposed, but by her own convinced acquiescence. In doing this may she have the cordial good-will of European governments, looking to see in her, not a reproduction of themselves, — which might well be but a deceitful imitation, — but an Asiatic people renewed from within by the power to which we ourselves owe all that we have — or, better, are. What maketh one to differ from another? Of the continued stable progress of European states there are two certain indications: one, in internal development, in individual growth; the other, in the tendency to external action, the cessation of which in a healthy, mature existence — national or personal — is the precursor of decay at hand, if not indeed the indication of decay already begun.

In Japan, and as yet in Japan alone, do we find the Asiatic welcoming European culture, in which, if a tree may fairly be judged by its fruit, is to be found the best prospect for the human race to realize the conditions most conducive to its happiness, — personal liberty, in due combination with restraints of law sufficient to, but not in excess of, the requirements of the general welfare. In this particular distinctiveness of characteristic, which has thus differentiated the receptivity of the Japanese from that of the continental Asiatic, we may perhaps see the influence of the insular environment that has permitted and favored the evolution of a strong national personality; and in the same condition we may not err in finding a promise of power to preserve and to propagate, by example and by influence, among those akin to her, the new polity which she has adopted, and by which she has profited, affording to them the example which she herself has found in the development of European peoples. The security and isolation of an insular position contributes, as nothing else can, to the strength of that quality in states which in men we call personality; and in states as in men no other quality is so influential. Nor should strength of personality be confounded with immobility, any more than firmness is identified with obstinacy. The persistence of Asia in its social conservatism has been passive; the strength of the rock it may be, but also that of vitality lost in petrification. Rocks neither grow nor flower; of themselves they change only by decay.

While the urgency of the present[1] conditions

[1] Written in early August, 1900.

in China, in which all the great European nations, with ourselves and Japan, have an equal concern, is evident, and constrains the action of the Powers to a common end, if not too concerted action, it is clear enough that only on the surface can there seem to be any departure, other than temporary, from the policy heretofore pursued by each state. In substantial, determinative conditions there has been no change. The outrage of Pekin and the tragedy of the Christian missionaries in China are merely a startling illustration of the possibilities which have all along been known to lurk under the surface; the more certainly because, as a rule, the Oriental, whether nation or individual, does not change. What has happened this year in China is just as likely, unless fear exercise its constraining force, to recur in the East now as it was a thousand years ago, because the East does not progress. With ourselves also like things, though on a smaller scale, happen now, revealing the brute that underlies us all; but they are far less frequent than five centuries past, they are less condoned, they are not the work of governments, nor usually of the more rational elements of our communities. They are most frequently the offspring of fears rooted in ignorance, also a condition not wholly unfamiliar in the more backward parts of civilized Christian states; but in none of these so universal in distribution, nor in such keeping with the general tone of society, from the government down, as in the ancient immobile civilizations of Asia.

Despite recent events in China, therefore, and the consequent momentary effect upon national action, — the momentary insistence of the short view, — there is no necessary change in the conditions which control national policies; because these, for the reasons given in the preceding papers, rest, primarily even, upon permanent conditions, chiefly external to China, and commensurate in extent with the compass of the globe from east to west. For the moment, a common wrong and a common danger have imposed upon the honor of nations the obligation of loyal, concerted action to avenge — not to revenge — the crime, and to exact surety for the future against recurrence; and for such surety nothing equals condign punishment for the past, — a lively sense, through experience, of disfavors to come in case of repeated offence. While such action is being taken, it becomes the nations — as it would honorable gentlemen or good citizens —

to sink political differences in mutual consideration, to cease from the competition of interests, until the common object demanded by the exigency of the moment has been accomplished by the enforcement of just retribution. But when this shall have been done, it will no longer be incumbent upon them to shut their eyes to facts and conditions which have not ceased to exist, and have only been temporarily superseded by circumstances of more immediate concern. It may, however, be profitable not to dismiss the recent past from consideration, before first observing that it has taught forcibly that mutual rivalry, — conflict of interest, — though a part of the truth, is but part; as towards Asia in its present conditions, Europe has learned that it has a community of interest, as well as a divergence. That community of interest may be defined as the need of bringing the Asian peoples within the compass of the family of Christian states; not by fetters and bands imposed from without, but by regeneration promoted from within. This principle, in intellectual appreciation and in practical observance, is perfectly compatible with the diligent safeguarding of individual national interest by precautions of whatsoever kind. It looks and works towards a far distant future, in which it sees, not a dream, but a goal, directive of a general course which meanwhile has to be continually accommodated to the exigencies of the passing day.

It is not too much to claim that the government of the United States, representing the national sovereignty which by our system rests in the great community of individual citizens, has not only recognized, but has, in its recent definition of its attitude, formulated, in express terms, both of these complementary and superficially contradictory ideas: the obligation of asserting our own rights and protecting our own interests against all comers, and, coincidently therewith, of respecting, not only the government of China, but the national individuality. It is perfectly consistent with this view of duty to assist both government and people to renew and confirm the national life; not by fussy interference on our part, but by generous sympathy, supplemented only as far as necessary by active support. And this declaration of our government is the more significant, because, while unquestionably elicited by recent occurrences, it expresses as its main motive a purpose of non-interference guaranteed by the general assent of our people through a long period of past years, to which it adds, by way of qualification, definitions of new duties and policies consequent upon novel conditions recently arisen. Herein is found combined, in close approach at least to a due proportion, both the idealism of rational statesmanship, which looks over and beyond the passing hour, joined to the practical capacity that adapts itself readily to the exigencies of the moment, modifying its action by them, as a seaman puts the helm down and goes about when an uncharted shoal appears ahead, resuming his course when he again sees the water clear in the direction he means to follow.

But while all this is true, and of most encouraging omen for the future in that it witnesses to the sagacity of our leadership in the past, it behooves us of the mass, who ultimately confirm or reject — and who therefore control — the action of those in authority, to look particularly to the coincidence and sequence of events during the few momentous years just gone by, in order that by studying the signs of the times we may understand at once the opportunities they extend and the consequent obligations they impose. This we owe, not to ourselves only, but to posterity, to which we hold the relation of a trustee to a ward. Our leaders, when a call for action comes, cannot outstrip by very much the recognized wishes of the people; and if these are to keep abreast of conditions, they must be at pains, not merely to comprehend them as they are, but to view them together, and to estimate tendency by indications. There is a double process: the observation of facts, and the rational deductions from them, — the data, and the practical conclusion drawn, which fixes the broad general lines of national determination. These established, and the support of the nation thus settled, details and daily management may be left to the government, strong before the world in the ascertained backing of its followers. The populace, which all we in the mass are, is often accused of fickleness; it is so, however, not from inherent instability, but because, where ignorance exists, conditions easily assume different appearances, and moods waver with the fleeting impressions thus produced. The remedy for this is solid understanding, obtained by mental toil.

What are the facts, summarily outlined? In the general progress of events it has come to pass, in this closing year of a century, that the commerce of the world — which implies as a main incident the utilization of the sea, the chief medium of commerce — has become the prize for which all the great states of the world are in competition. Some, possibly, do not expect ever to be leaders; but all either wish a greater share than they now have, or at the least to preserve their present proportion. This includes not only the power to produce, — mainly an internal question, — but the power to exchange freely throughout as large a section of the world's population as can be reached. In this competition the most of states are, as a matter of policy, unwilling to trust entirely to the operation of what we may call — not quite accurately — natural forces. The race as hitherto run, or the particular conditions of some more favored nations, — the United States, for example, so richly dowered with the raw material of wealth, and with energy to use it, — have resulted in giving some a start which puts the remainder at a disadvantage, if the issue is left to purely commercial causes; to superiority in quantity or quality of production, for instance, or to greater ability of management, either in intelligence or economy. Issues determined in this manner are more solid, but they require time longer than impatience wishes to concede; hence, the desire to hasten prosperity by extending territorial control and reserving to one's self commercial advantage in the regions mastered. This result may be reached either by direct annexation, or by preponderant political influence; but both these mean, ultimately, physical force, exerted or potential, and this generates opposing force, averse from allowing its own people to be deprived by such means. Thus competition becomes conflict, the instrument of which is not commercial emulation, but military power — land or sea.

In Europe and in America territorial occupancy is now politically fixed and guaranteed, so far as broad lines are concerned. Any changes of boundaries now possible, if effected, would produce no material result in universal commercial conditions. Australasia also is occupied, and the political dependence of the islands of the sea has been determined by arrangements between civilized states, more or less artificial, but internationally final. The huge continent of Africa, with exceptions small and inconsequential relatively to its area, is in the same condition. Its commercial relations, therefore, will be prescribed by states whose established right to do so will not be contested. Moreover, in the regard of commerce, the fewness and backwardness of its inhabitants as yet make Africa a field of minor importance.

There remains, therefore, Asia, the conditions of which from the stand-point of world politics have been the subject under investigation in the preceding papers. The results of the discussion in them conducted are embodied in certain broad conclusions which, for the sake of further consideration, especially as touching the policy of the United States, should here be summarized. As a consequence of analysis, it was seen that the portion of Asia which is as yet in a position of political instability, and therefore open to serious change by foreign influences, lies mainly between 30° and 40° north latitude, a belt of six hundred miles width, within which are the greater part of Turkey in Asia, of Persia, of Afghanistan, and of the Chinese Empire, including much of the valley of the Yang-tse-Kiang, the great central region of China. North and south of the parallels mentioned, a decisively preponderant and well established political power rests in the hands, respectively, of Russia and of Great Britain; the one dependent mainly upon the land, the other upon the sea, for the element of military force upon which commercial control depends, when exclusive possession is either sought or resisted. It was pointed out that the whole question of control of commerce with the far East by political intrusion — viewed apart from the question of competition by purely commercial methods — really turned, in the actual conditions of the civilized world, upon the competing forces of land and of sea power. In the problem of Asia, and within the limits of the continent, these factors of military strength find their local representation in Russia and in Great Britain, two states which also possess in numbers, relatively to the whole world, the greatest army and greatest navy, and the commercial methods of which present probably the sharpest contrasts between freedom of trade and despotic exclusion, either by absolute prohibition or insurmountable preference.

It was further argued, however, that the territorial positions of the other great states, — including the United States, — being exterior to the continent, threw them necessarily upon sea power, so far as military force in the further

East is concerned, ranging them therefore alongside of Great Britain in general purpose, though by no means consequently in formal alliance. Not only their methods, but their objects, must resemble hers; for like her, owing to their geographical remoteness and imperative interests in other parts of the world, they are deficient in disposable means for readily projecting their military power inland in China. This defect, though obvious enough before, is now receiving convincing illustration. It applies less forcibly to the United States than to Europe, because by our shortest route we are nearer; because the ocean, ministering so powerfully to our defence, liberates us proportionately for external action; because our numbers are so great and increasing; and because our Asian base in the Philippines, being insular, and as distant from Europe as China itself, shares the defensive quality of our own land. Nevertheless, the width of the Pacific, like the distance of South Africa from Great Britain, imposes upon such military efforts a difficulty which must ever disincline us to them, when avoidable. Japan is near, but the limits of her area place limits upon population and resultant wealth, which must long restrict her power.

For the reasons given, the desire of all these states must be to effect their commercial aims, not by show of military force, still less by violence, but by motives of advantage, mutual to themselves and China, of which commerce and its gains, though not the worthiest or most benignant result, are the most obvious and convincing expression. In its train we may hope will follow those moral and spiritual ideals, the appropriation of which outweighs material well-being in the thought of those who believe that man does not live by bread only, and in which alone can surely be found the happy renewal of Asia. So far therefore as there is, or is likely to be, contest for pre-eminence in Asia, and specifically in China, the states concerned — except Russia, and possibly France, because of her alliance with Russia — are driven perforce to throw themselves chiefly upon sea power in the broadest sense of the word. On the one side sea power is represented by maritime commerce, by which, and by which alone, they expect themselves to benefit, and by reciprocity of benefit to influence China. On the other side it is by sea power in the military sense, — of navies, and of action on the seaboard and navigable waters, — that they must maintain their position and rights in the trade of China in case the attempt is made, whether by gradual encroachment or by instant violence, to exclude them in whole or in part, or to fetter their freedom of access. In view of the possibility of such an attempt, the military and political features of the general situation have been discussed in the previous papers, and, with a single exception, need no repetition of emphasis here.

That single exception is the stream and valley of the Yang-tse-Kiang. Its importance is, in the eyes of the writer, sufficiently great, both in the commercial and political sense, to warrant some further insistence. This need be at no great length, just because, when once stated, the conditions are too clear to require enlargement. The stream penetrates far inland, and through a controlling part of its course is accessible directly from the sea by very large vessels. The valley, in its broadest comprehension, depends upon the river for its readiest intercourse with the outside world, and it intervenes geographically between northern and southern China, whether for distribution of merchandize or for operations of war. Influence established there possesses, consequently, the advantages of the interior position, and of open and constant communication, through the river, with its base — the sea. Preponderant commercial importance and a climate comparatively moderate reinforce the advantages resultant upon the other conditions, and the whole constitutes this central, east and west, section of the Empire by far the most considerable of all in political possibilities. For these reasons the outer world of maritime states can most readily and beneficently act upon China in this quarter, and China herself can hence distribute the benefits she receives more widely and evenly throughout her area. Seed sown here will yield a hundredfold, as to thirtyfold elsewhere.

The expansion of commerce, and the benefit resulting therefrom, are, however, only part of the objects that necessitate European pressure upon the China of our day. The close approach and contact of Eastern and Western civilization, and the resultant mutual effects, are matters which can no longer be disregarded, or postponed by any arguments derived from the propriety of non-interference, or from the conventional rights of a so-called independent state to regulate its own internal affairs. They have ceased to be its own in the sense of Chinese isolation. Contact and interaction have begun; the process can neither be turned back nor arrested. All that can profitably be attempted is to direct, by so shaping conditions that the higher elements of either civilization can act as freely as do the motives of pecuniary profit which, though perfectly proper, are lower as well as stronger. As the nations have insisted that we shall be allowed to sell and to buy, without pretending that the Chinese subject should be compelled to trade with us, leaving his personal action free to the motives of gain that operate with mankind; so they will have to insist that currency be permitted to our ideas, liberty to exchange thought in Chinese territory with the individual Chinaman, though equally without any compulsion resting upon him to listen even, much less to embrace. There is no tenable argument against the latter demand that does not equally hold against the former. On the contrary, if the advantage to us is great of a China open to commerce, the danger to us and to her is infinitely greater of a China enriched and strengthened by the material advantages we have to offer, but uncontrolled in the use of them by any clear understanding, much less any full acceptance, of the mental and moral forces which have generated and in large measure govern our political and social action. Our failure perfectly to realize in practice our principles in such matters does not invalidate the merit of the principle, nor negative the fact that we do derive benefit even from imperfect conformity. We get less good, doubtless, than we should, and could, but for our dereliction from our standards; but the appeal can confidently be made to history that those faithful to the ideas have been the leaven that has worked effectually so far, even though much yet remains for it to accomplish.

It would appear then that the principal objects to be kept in view in dealing with the Chinese question, are, 1. Prevention of preponderant political control by any one external state, or group of states; and, 2. Insistence upon the open door, in a broader sense than that in which the phrase is commonly used; that is, the door should be open not only for commerce, but also for the entrance of European thought and its teachers in its various branches, when they seek admission voluntarily, and not as agents of a foreign government. Not only is the influence of the thinker superior in true value to the mere gain of commerce, but also there is actual danger to the European family of nations, in case China should develop an organized strength whence has been excluded the corrective and elevating element of the higher ideals, which in Europe have made good their controlling influence over mere physical might. Rationally, from this point of view, there is much that is absurd in the outcry raised against missionary effort, as a thing incompatible with peaceful development and progress. Christianity and Christian teaching are just as really factors in the mental and moral equipment of European civilization as any of the philosophical or scientific processes that have gone to build up the general result. Opinions differ as to the character and degree of the influence of Christianity, in estimates qualitative and quantitative, but the fact of influence cannot be denied. From the purely political standpoint Christian thought and teaching have just the same right — no less, if no more — to admission into China as any other form of European activity, commercial or intellectual. Nor is the fact of offence taken by classes of Chinamen a valid argument for exclusion. The building of a railroad is not a distinctively Christian act, but it offends large numbers of Chinese, who are nevertheless compelled to acquiesce if their government consent; whereas the consent of the Chinese government to missionary effort will compel no Chinaman to listen to a Christian teacher. Every step forward in the march that has opened China to trade has been gained by pressure; the most important have been the result of actual war. Commerce has won its way by violence, actual or feared; thought, both secular and Christian, asks only freedom of speech.

Conceding the critical importance of the present moment in the history of the world, admitting that movements intellectual and political, long in progress in China, are now reaching a turning point determinative of great future issues, it is essential to the United States that her individual citizens should seriously consider, and within themselves settle, the part the country ought to play, and the preparation necessary to that part. There is the preparation of purpose, and there is the preparation of power. Preparation of purpose is a mental and moral process, resulting in conviction as to right and wrong, followed by the conscious adoption of a course of action, — the formation of a policy, — general in outline but definite in object. Preparation of power is a material act, and consists of two correlative elements, viz.: 1. Provision of force, to the extent needed; and, 2. Curtailment of obligation, — of responsibility, — actual or contingent, present or promissory, in direction and in amount, beyond that which is demanded by the clear necessities of the political conditions. In short, economy of exertion, because it husbands strength, is the complement of the process of development which creates or augments strength.

Our policy and our power, therefore, are the two leading lines upon which consideration and reflection must concentrate their energy. As towards the immense world question, commensurate only with international relations in their widest sense, of which China is the central issue, the general world conditions upon which policies should turn have been the subject of study in the preceding papers. The elements of the problem, — of the political strategy, — as seen by the author, have in them been indicated. As towards China herself, and, in particular, the recent astounding events have drawn from our government a declaration, of purpose and of principles, which may fairly be said to represent a policy realized in our past action, and to affirm it for the present and future. Our people have not now to evolve a policy, but to decide whether that of the past justifies itself to their conscience, to their sense of right and wrong, and embodies their purpose of the present. This still existent policy may, I apprehend, fairly be stated to be the determination to have equal commercial privileges, and withal to respect to the utmost the integrity of Chinese territory, and the individuality of the Chinese character in shaping its own government and polity. We meddle not with their national affairs until they become internationally unendurable.

But in the very enunciation of this policy we are confronted by the fact that it is diverse from that of some other states, as shown by their acts in special instances, and plausibly to be inferred from their general course and obvious tendency. Such divergence is not always necessarily a cause for alarm, but it is for watchfulness; and it must be taken into account, as an element influential upon our own policy, not perhaps in general conception or as towards China, but in the matter of deciding upon the preparation we need, and the freehandedness to be maintained in external relations of lesser importance. Needless external preoccupations might greatly embarrass us, in case divergence from our policy should develop into opposition to our interests, or to those of civilization in general.

Briefly, we cannot be sure of the commercial advantages known as the "open door," unless we are prepared to do our share in holding it open. We cannot count upon respect for the territory of China, unless we are ready to throw, not only our moral influence, but, if necessity arise, our physical weight into the conflict to resist an expropriation, the result of which might be to exclude our commerce and neutralize our influence. Our influence we believe,—and have a right to believe,—is for good; it is the influence of a nation which respects the right of peoples to shape their own destinies, pushing even to exaggeration its belief in their ability to do so. But it is vain to hope for national influence in China, unless representative Chinese recognize—not only integrity of our purpose towards themselves, but—our evident ability and intention to support them against demands which overpass reasonable limits, having regard not to our own immediate interests only, but to the general interest of the world, from which we cannot dissociate ourselves in this matter without ultimate national injury. Such limits may not be capable of precise definition, before an occasion arises; but that a general principle, satisfactory as a guide in our own general action, and for general understanding by others, can be affirmed, is evidenced by the clear tenor of the recent declaration of our government communicated to foreign capitals.

To those who are able to receive it, — and I believe there are many, — I would say that it is impossible for our government — which is our people — to allow the question of China, in the stage which it has now reached, to drift at the sport of circumstances. That China should develop normally from within, by willing acceptance and gradual appropriation of sounder political views and higher intellectual ideals, is right. Nations cannot be born, or reborn, in a day; nor can the raw material of individual men, personally excellent, be manufactured into a living national organism by mere external pressure. Growth processes are from within and presume antecedent vitality, inherent or imparted. But vigor for self-renewal, or to receive and assimilate nutriment from without, unforced or unaided, does not constitute the condition of China to-day, as it did constitute, approximately at least, that of Japan a half-century ago; though even Japan has owed to external pressure the opportunity of which she has richly availed herself, but which she certainly did not seek of her own initiative. China not only has repelled, as Japan once did, but after long years of contact and opportunity she continues to repel the admission of the leaven which alone can permeate and vivify her deadness. The reactionary movement in progress at the present moment[1] aims at severing communication with the only possible source of real life. It is permissible, nay, incumbent, to resist it; to insist, in the general interest, by force if need be, that China remain open to action by European and American processes of life and thought. She may not — cannot — be forced to drink, but she must at least allow the water to be brought to her people's doors. If the United States stands wholly aside, this work will be done all the same, lacking only our individual contribution to it. Can we without responsibility to

[1] Written August 10, 1900. The relief force reached Pekin August 15.

God and man decline our aid, which our respect for nationality and personality — carried at times to an excess even absurd — will render especially disinterested, as well as especially helpful through the confidence it commands?

The part offered to us is great, the urgency is immediate, and the preparation made for us, rather than by us, in the unwilling acquisition of the Philippines, is so obvious as to embolden even the least presumptuous to see in it the hand of Providence. Our highest authority, while rebuking rash judgment, rebukes also with at least equal severity the failure to read the signs of the times. This, therefore, we must seek to do. Our decision is momentous, in view of the possibilities involved in acceptance or in refusal, and of the wide range of interests and duties to be considered and co-ordinated in counting the cost of either course. Decision is the preparation of purpose; the cost embraces both the preparation of power and all that is involved in its future exertion, as far as we can foresee. And in order to the due running of the race before us, to the full exhibition of strength at decisive points, it is necessary to lay aside every unnecessary weight, to put away from ourselves, even at some sacrifice, cherished prepossessions, long-standing prejudices, which, if retained, would futilely disseminate our force. What One has called the single eye, and Napoleon phrased as exclusiveness of purpose, is a necessary condition of effective action.

Assuming our resolution to maintain our commercial rights and to exert influence in China, by encouraging and supporting native action, though not by any assumption of authority or acquisition of territory, the valley of the Yang-tse is clearly indicated as the central scene of our general interest, however we may be momentarily diverted, as by the recent occurrences in Pekin, to action different in character and direction from our fixed usual policy. The open door, both for commerce and for intellectual interaction, should be our aim everywhere in China; but it can most easily be compassed in this middle region, and there find the surest foundation for impression upon other parts, because there sea power can most solidly establish itself. The very fact that sea-going steamers can go as far as Hankow, six hundred miles from the sea, and thence take cargoes, without shifting bulk, to any great port of the world, shows without further insistence that this valley is the decisive field where commerce, the energizer of material civilization, can work to greatest advantage, and can most certainly receive the support of the military arm of sea power, which, where force enters into world politics, is the main reliance of the Teutonic peoples. It must also for some time to come be the main reliance of the Chinese people in resistance to foreign domination, as distinguished from legitimate foreign influence.

Our attention in the farther East thus localized, concentrated, for the very reason that effort seeking to cover a given area works more advantageously from a centre than by dispersion at points of a circumference, we shall find ourselves one of several powers rivals in interest,—competitors,—with the danger, incident to competition, of degenerating into antagonism. The fact does not call upon us to circumscribe our independence of action by formal alliance with one, or declared opposition to another; but it does demand that we rid our minds of the caricature of independence, which receives frequent expression in words, probably because it reflects a condition of our popular consciousness. Each man and each state is independent just so far as there is strength to go alone, and no farther. When this limit is reached, if farther steps must be made, co-operation must be accepted. In that case the only certain foundation for harmony of action and continuance of relations is to be found in common interests and common habits of thought. Where the latter are traditional, striking their roots deep in the past, community of ideas and identity of action in matters of right and wrong become most probable. Of all the nations we shall meet in the East, Great Britain is the one with which we have by far the most in common in the nature — not in the identity — of our interests there, and in our standards of law and justice. Co-operation, therefore, is indicated; but it is a mistake to assume that co-operation, which act by act is voluntary, necessitates or implies abnegation of that moral responsibility, involved in freedom of choice at each moment, in the retention and observance of which alone is real independence of action preserved, and which a treaty — of alliance, or of arbitration, if unconditioned — may impair culpably, because it pledges the unknown future. Hereabouts lies the fallacy of much popular oratory on more than one subject.

To assure the open door in its fullest sense, requires power in evidence, not merely localized in China itself, but asserted over the maritime lines of communication; especially over the shortest. This inevitable extension of effort shows at once the necessity of co-operation among states; of division of labor, mutually, if tacitly, recognized. In the antagonism of policy between land and sea power which now exists, no one nation of those dependent upon the latter is competent to develop and sustain the whole gigantic scheme. Narrowed down even to the decisive points, which all control must be in politics as in war, the task overpasses the strength of any one state.

In final analysis the great lines of communication to the farther East are two, from Europe and from America. The former is by way of Suez, the latter by the Pacific; but the present distribution of our national wealth, and its communications with our seaboard, require, and doubtless will insure, the opening of access for our Atlantic slope by way of the Central American Isthmus. In that case the American line of communications to China may be correctly said to be by Nicaragua, — or Panama, — as that of Europe is by way of Suez; and as the

Mediterranean, Egypt, Asia Minor, the Red Sea, and Aden, designate the points decisive of control by the one route, so do the Caribbean Sea and the continental surroundings of the future canal, with Hawaii and the Philippines, fix those of the other, the importance of which to ourselves make it our especial interest.

That it should be our special interest, however, is not all. It is also our charge, from the standpoint of international relations, as well as from that of our duty to the present and future of our own country. I do not mean here to affirm an obligation of benevolence to other nations, strong enough to take care of themselves. I mean, on the contrary, that because of great common interests — with Great Britain especially, though not solely — in the Pacific commerce of the future, and in the nature of the development of China, we need to receive and to give support, and should be ashamed to receive more than we give, in proportion to our means and opportunities. Gradually, as we have grown in strength, we have made good our claims to preponderant consideration in the Caribbean and at the Isthmus; we have obtained acquiescence where we once met opposition — from Great Britain herself. Is this a mere selfish, and in so far barren, triumph of national diplomacy, or an opportunity involving further duty? Certainly the latter; not because British welfare, regarded alone, is a concern for our action, but because community of interests, and duty to the world's future, centring about China, impose mutual support. This cannot be assured in matters pertaining to the East merely by accord localized there. It requires also such a grip upon our special great line of communications thither, from both our coasts, as shall give assurance that the force of our distant action cannot be impaired by any weakening of a link essential to its continuity.

From the conditions, we must be in effective naval force in the Pacific. We must similarly be in effective force on the Atlantic; not for the defence of our coasts primarily, or immediately, as is commonly thought, — for in warfare, however much in defence of right, the navy is not immediately an instrument of defence but of offence, — but because the virtual predominance of our naval power in the Caribbean is essential to preserve the use of the Isthmian Canal to our commerce, and to give our navy quick access to the Pacific.

We are confronted, in short, with the necessity of providing a weight that shall be decisive — or at least shall contribute largely to decisiveness — in both the Pacific and the Caribbean. It is obvious that, to be decisive, weight is not always necessarily a great weight, but depends upon the already existing relative conditions of the opposing scales. The conditions now, however, are not such that an inconsiderable naval force on our part can secure for us the consideration we naturally think due us in the councils of the world, nor discharge the obligations incumbent upon us as a member of the family of states, whose interests, often conflicting, must be adjusted on a basis of righteousness, and so maintained by demonstration of power. Our calculations must also take into account the fact that, when the canal is in operation, our Pacific and Atlantic fleets can communicate for mutual support only by an artificial route, too easily interrupted. This loses us in great measure the military advantage of an interior line, which a natural strait would give; the advantage by which a force centrally situated operates effectually in two directions, reinforcing the situation in the one or the other, as needed. Thus a navy of consideration at Malta can act towards Gibraltar or Suez — the way is open as far as the water is concerned, the question therefore is one of force only; but at Suez the power to act towards both India and the Mediterranean depends not upon military force alone, but upon the canal being open. Suez, however, being on the natural level throughout, is much less easily susceptible of prolonged interruption than a canal dependent upon locks, as any Central American canal must be.

As, therefore, for the exertion of our commercial and moral influence in the East it is of pressing importance to bring our Atlantic slope into close communication by a canal at the Isthmus, — which will serve our material interests, moreover, in other ways, — so it is of equal importance that we assure the use of the canal, once there, by the solidity of our naval position in the Caribbean. But, as this is a military question, let there here be interposed the caution, than which none is more clearly written on the pages of military history, that substantial security does not mean absolute security. There is no such thing in war as absolute certainty; risk cannot be eliminated wholly from any military situation, whether of passive defence or of offensive action. I suppose it is much the same in all callings; but for war certainly a reasonable preponderance of chances in one's favor is all that can be assured. Napoleon has asserted this in almost identical words in one of his pithy phrases.

May we then dismiss the effort for probable security because we cannot have absolute? Do men do so in any circumstances? Certainly not successful men. Let us then consider what conditions, if realized, would give the best prospect of preserving to our use the Isthmian Canal. The first, without which all others are of no avail, is our own strength, demonstrated by a fleet available for immediate action there, of power great enough — not to overcome any naval force that might conceivably be brought against us, for that would be beyond our means, but — to make it evidently inexpedient, politically, for the greatest navy to contest our predominance in the Caribbean. This insures us, by a single military provision, a primacy of consideration which will result in the prevalence of our policy and, in direct consequence of our policy so maintained, in the security of the canal; which, it should be repeated, is an essential element of our influence in the Pacific and in China. The provision of the fleet, however, is the first step, without which the others cannot follow.

Now the only Power that in the past has been seriously disposed to contest this preponderance has been Great Britain. The West Indies and South America have till very lately been with her controlling objects of commercial, and therefore of political, consideration. This attitude has been largely traditional from the eighteenth century, when the sugar of the one was a chief item of her trade, and the once Spanish colonies of the other presented a coveted field for exploitation, estimated then much as China is now. Forty or fifty years ago, therefore, we were directly antagonized in the Caribbean by the nation having the strongest navy in the world, and convinced that our policy — in brief the Monroe Doctrine — was irreconcileable with her interests. The events of the last half century have changed this, and, what is more important, Great Britain, though within but a very few years, now recognizes the change. The West Indies, which in the opening years of this expiring century entertained one-fourth of British commerce, are become a factor relatively insignificant; and while South America has not wholly disappointed the hopes of former days, its development has not kept pace with the interests that have grown up elsewhere.

We find, therefore, on the part of the greatest of naval states, a politic disposition to acquiesce in our naval predominance in the Caribbean; and this disposition is bound to increase, because it rests securely upon two facts that will remain permanent for a time far beyond the horizon of this generation. These facts are, first, that Great Britain's interests elsewhere are so great that she must unload herself of responsibility for the Caribbean, and, second, that some of the principal among those major interests of hers are so evidently coincident in character with ours, that we cannot but follow, though perfectly independently, the same general line of policy, and in so doing support her. It is, therefore, her interest that we remain strong, and since an essential element of our strength is in the Caribbean, we may prudently reckon upon the moral support of Great Britain in any political clash with other nations there, unless we take a stand morally indefensible.

There is no reason seriously to doubt that just

such support was given during the late war with Spain. On the contrary, the writer has been assured, by an authority in which he entirely trusts, that to a proposition made to Great Britain, to enter into a combination to constrain the use of our power, — as Japan was five years ago constrained by the joint action of Russia, France, and Germany, — the reply was not only a passive refusal to enter into such combination, but an assurance of active resistance to it, if attempted. If actions speak louder than words, such a fact outweighs paragraphs of demonstration of future probabilities, based though this be upon the clearest arguments from existing conditions. Call such an attitude friendship, or policy, as you will, — the name is immaterial; the fact is the essential thing and will endure, because it rests upon solid interests. Not every saying of Washington is as true now as it was when uttered, and some have been misapplied; but it is just as true now as ever, that it is vain to expect governments to act continuously on any other ground than national interest. They have no right to do so, being agents and not principals.

Moral support, expressed in popular bias, and resting upon community of interest and of political standards, is a weighty political factor. It carries with it not only the force of opinion, but uncertainty on the part of an antagonist as to whether moral support may not become material; whether the cold friend may not at short notice become the hot ally. Great Britain no longer has occasion to feel antagonism towards us in the Caribbean, and any traditional sentiment of that sort which may remain in her older men must disappear from popular consciousness, because contradicted by the facts. Antagonism, resting once on real opposition of interest, is being displaced by realization of the community of interest known as the open door, and of community in political principles, the outgrowth of traditions which, having been not stagnant but progressive, have now by evolution reached the stage of willing the integrity of China and its free development from within. From this, it is but a short step to a national support of China against foreign domination, or annexation, or partition,—a policy identical in principle with the Monroe Doctrine; but to take this, either state needs a reasonable security of the other's co-operation. As far as community of interest and of standard goes, the assurance is there, nor is the evidence of national feeling absent; but there is wanting on our part the assurance of the national purpose, — not by compact, but by action, — of which action a first instalment is the provision of force. We cannot expect the nations, friendly or the reverse, to take our purpose seriously, unless they see us firm in provision as well as in speech.

It may be objected, in Great Britain as well as here, that if there be among some of our citizens a clear appreciation of the advantage of common, though mutually independent, action, there is in very many of us a loudly expressed bitterness of feeling towards her; and that this will impede, if not prevent, mutual support in external matters of common interest. It is possible to admit the fact of the bitterness expressed, without accepting the conclusion. Sentiment is mighty, mightier at moments than interest; but where interest rests on real and permanent conditions, and sentiment on impressions which are transient and unreal, there can be no doubt which will prevail with the victory ever won by truth. The interest is real. The open door expresses a policy as important to us as to Great Britain; more important to us than to her, if our export trade take on the superior proportions anticipated by some serious thinkers. The standards also really exist. We, like her, and she, like us, at the present time shrink from partition and annexation as evils, — evil in principle, and evil in the consequent burden entailed. Despite current prejudice diligently fostered, it will at no distant day be recognized also by our people that the annexation of the Boer republics was a measure forced upon Great Britain, as the annexation of the Philippines has been upon ourselves, and as was the annexation, against its will, a generation ago, of the Southern Confederacy; regardless of the fact that it then possessed all the elements of a *de facto* government, resting upon the willing allegiance of the great majority of the inhabitants. The sentiment in the United States which to-day withstands movement in the direction of our common interests is partly traditional, like that which survives in Great Britain concerning the Caribbean; partly, as is notorious, it is the transference to United States politics of foreign prepossessions by citizens foreign-born, in their own persons or in those of their parents. Such sentiment is transient; for it is unreal in that it does not correspond to the facts of the United States' interests. A sagacious statesman will see in this the assurance of the ultimate trend of sentiment. But such an one will also reckon, with very different certitude, upon our national backwardness to provide the organized force, — especially the naval, — without which the attempted expression of national will, on emergency, becomes the clumsy and abortive gestures of a flabby and untrained giant.

To pronounce definitely upon the amount of such force is either to utter a dogmatic personal opinion, or to enter upon a prolonged technical discussion unsuitable to this paper and occasion. To indicate its general character and its points of application is another matter; for quality, as distinct from quantity, rests upon general considerations, which, being at once few and obvious, may be readily summarized and, whether accepted or rejected, readily understood.

The Atlantic, north of the equator, is the ocean of that old community of European civilization upon which, from our point of view, the welfare of humanity rests. Interior to this community the boundaries of the great states are, in leading outline, so fixed and recognized that, — whatever clashes may arise over external interests, — there is no probability of large changes of territorial possession and consequent local political control.

The Pacific is different; it is a new-comer into broad world interests. As the Atlantic some four centuries ago, with the widening outlook that followed the discovery of America and of the Cape of Good Hope, succeeded to the central position once held by the Mediterranean, so now the last half century — it is scarcely more — has received in the course of events its discovery, its revelation, of conditions which existed indeed, as did America before Columbus, but had been as yet unknown, because unappreciated. And upon the discovery has followed the apprehension of what is to happen when the barriers are breaking down between two civilizations which stand upon such different levels — politically, economically, socially, and in standards moral and intellectual — as do the West and the East.

In estimating the issue, it is difficult to exaggerate the importance, as a factor, of that particular type of political freedom, of aptitude for self-government, and of tenacious adherence to recognized law — by which alone freedom and self-government consist with orderly progress — that has been embodied in the race loosely called Anglo-Saxon. This type has proved its vitality and its worth by continuous existence and consistent development, from the home of its origin, on the continental shores of the North Sea, throughout its abode in Great Britain, and in its subsequent transplantation to the over-sea countries which have now become the United States and the self-governing colonies of the British Empire. These traditions, remaining ever the same in general idea, have been translated into particular action by the hundred successive generations that have applied them to their own conditions, as these varied from age to age. Thus progressing, they have in our day reached a development, in principles and methods, the due influence of which upon the future, by consistent political support, is the charge alike of Great Britain and the United States. For, play with words and facts as we may, assert the composite character of the population of the United States, — which none will deny, — the truth remains that the strength of our people as of Great Britain, — herself a congeries of races, — rests in the common political and legal tradition, preserved and intensified under conditions of separation nothing less than insular, which both have inherited by unbroken transmission from the old home, where the forefathers of the one race dwelt when history first knew them. This type, by its virile power of adaptation, has not only predominated over, but absorbed and assimilated, all other social and racial types with which it has been brought into political association. Many magicians stood before Pharaoh, but Aaron's rod swallowed all the others.

To the full expression of this political force, great alike in its nobility and in its vitality, the United States owes to mankind her due contribution; for in it is one of the greatest hopes — in our own national opinion the very greatest hope — of humanity. A great door and an effectual is here open to us, and it is needless to say that there are many adversaries. And if to such contribution is essential the dismissal of old prepossessions, the recognition of facts hitherto not understood, resulting in a co-operation which shall not sacrifice independence of conscience by pledges, — whether of alliance or of arbitration, — this price should be cheerfully paid; as should be also that of any other exertion within our reasonable power to make.

The sphere for our external exertion in this cause is clearly indicated as the Pacific and the East, incident to which is predominance in the

Caribbean by a navy of such size that, with Great Britain eliminated as a probable opponent, — because of the radical changes in world conditions and of the coincidence of our interests with hers in the great questions of the near future, — and with her support indicated to the extent of the interests common to her and to us, we need have no substantial reason to apprehend interference there. The consideration here advanced bears so heavily upon the national advantage, in the matter not only of security but of expense in needed preparation, — if Great Britain should be considered as a probable enemy instead of a probable ally, — that it becomes a matter of patriotic duty to every citizen to consider whether he does well to cherish old animosities; to reflect whether the period in which, historically, these prejudices have their rise is not now as wholly past as the voyage of Columbus; or whether, perchance, they are simply transplanted to our soil from Europe by a process — in that case most misnamed — of naturalization. It is no true naturalization which grafts upon our politics sentiments drawn from abroad, and foreign to our interests or duties.

Relations between Great Britain and ourselves

that rested upon mutual understanding of common interests and common traditions would far exceed in potential force any formal alliance,— which for many reasons would be greatly to be deprecated. The perception of community of interest involves also inevitably the recognition of opposition, not only in form, but in spirit, inherent in other political systems with which in Asia we shall be brought into contact, — possibly into collision. The two considerations — coincidence of interest on the one side, and opposition of political methods on the other — would each have a just weight in determining the measure of our naval preparation, and would modify seriously, in the writer's apprehension, the application of the principle by him stated only four years ago, by which the amount of our naval force should be determined.[1] The principle is not affected. If correct then, as I believe, it is correct now; but there is in my mind no question that national policies have since then so developed, and international relations consequently so changed, that application to the new conditions will necessarily give a new result. We are forced now, in considering the national attitude proper to be as-

[1] Interest of American Sea Power, pp. 179–181.

sumed, to dismiss from mind the nearer past, — because, from its very closeness, it confuses the sense of proportion, — and to throw ourselves back upon the remote past, upon the origins of institutions, and upon the national spirit embodied in them, in order to recognize what are our real affinities, which should rightly and profitably direct our action in the immediate future.

In our calculations as to our necessary preparations under such conditions, it would not be presuming an unfair burden to Great Britain to reckon in part upon her supreme navy as a factor in a possible co-operation, and division of labor. It would be so only if we grudged our due proportion of a naval effort tending to the common advantage. Community of interest in objects implies mutual interest in each other's strength. To Great Britain the navy she maintains is indispensable to national safety, to the British Islands as such, and to the integrity of the widely dispersed British Empire. Whatsoever relations to other states she may temporarily entertain, this she must always have; while on the other hand she is at no such need of internal development as still weighs heavily upon our national resources.

Contrary to her, we need not to fear vital injury by an external blow to our communications with the world. For simple internal safety and maintenance we can depend upon ourselves, and we have no distant possessions vital to our mere existence, however useful they may be to our external development and influence. But in the great future of the world to which our political conditions seem to call upon us to co-operate, for the good of both and of the world at large, each is interested to see the other grow in strength. There need, therefore, be no captiousness on the part of Great Britain, nor any mortification on our part, if the proportions of military navy which we could contribute to the common end be modest, compared to hers, and that we devote resources to a development of national internal vigor which will inure to the common strength. The two efforts will be not contradictory, but complementary.

Our fleet must, however, be adequate, keeping in view the amount of support to which Great Britain would be limited by her extensive responsibilities. It must be adequate, considering those who might oppose us, whether in the East or in the Caribbean. It must be adequate, considering that on account of our merely national interests, as represented by our two ocean coasts, we must be able to exert naval power in both the Pacific and the Atlantic, remembering, also, that the future canal, while facilitating support between our fleets on either side, is nevertheless open to interruption by force or treachery. As regards other nations, the principle before alluded to is not affected; it is merely modified by the differing positions now occupied by Great Britain and by ourselves, brought about chiefly by the recognition of changes and events in the East.

Insistence, however, should be laid upon one element of naval strength, which in mention is so usually omitted that it is reasonable to infer that it is most inadequately appreciated. We hear much of ships built, and of the mechanical results attained in them, as evidenced by speed, gun-power, armor, etc.; but we hear rarely of our great deficiency in trained men to run these machines in their various forms, — for a gun is a machine quite as really as the propelling power of a vessel. To meet this defect, which is not only actual but great, there is no resource but the maintenance of a standing force of enlisted men, as well as of commissioned officers. A hundred years ago, when the engines were sails and guns simple tubes, the merchant seaman was already an engineer, and the gun handling was easily acquired; indeed merchant ships also not infrequently carried cannon. There was, therefore, a large recruiting ground of efficient men always at hand, though bitter experience showed how the commerce of the country could suffer from such heavy drafts upon its seamen.

This resource no longer exists. A certain proportion of the engine-room force may possibly be drawn from the merchant service, but for the gun handling, upon which the fate of war depends, the deck hand of the merchant steamer is useless for intelligent action; he can do no more, at the most critical moment of opening hostilities, then pull and haul. It is a safe generalization to say that not more than one-third of a ship's company in war can safely be composed of such material. Therefore, to calculate the standing force of a navy, in peace and for war, the rule would be to estimate the fixed force, on a war footing, for each ship on the list, built or building. Two-thirds of the total obtained by adding these several results, would represent the size of the standing force, the established personnel, of the fleet in peace. When war arises, the other third may be sought outside.

Coincidently with the development of our power, we should, in order to effectiveness of action, consider also the retrenchment of responsibility. Briefly, this remark is intended to raise the question, in view of the tremendous advance in importance of the Pacific and Asia, whether the extension of the Monroe Doctrine to the extent of supporting the independence of the states of extreme South America against all European interference, is a position now either wise or tenable? Great Britain suffers many strains by the dispersion of her Empire, but it is at least *her* Empire, — bone of her bone and flesh of her flesh. But what part have we, naturally or politically, in the foreign communities — foreign in blood and in tradition — south of the valley of the Amazon. That they do not love us is notorious; probably, indeed, they love us less because of our supposed purpose of interposition, which they doubtless would welcome in a strait, but which in ordinary times causes them chiefly mortification and apprehension. Within range of effect upon the Isthmus, certainly, our clear interest forbids toleration of any acquisition, through possession or through influence, by a great foreign state — more so now than ever before; but for the American communities beyond that range, our professed political concern is to us a waste of strength, as it is to them distasteful. The great valley of the Amazon, not unlike that of the Yang-tse, though far more practicable, indicates easily a great commercial zone in which the "open door" might profitably be assured by international understanding, and which also might very wisely be accepted in our national consciousness as interposing a broad effectual belt between the region where the Monroe Doctrine is applicable, and that where, for any useful purpose, it ceases to apply.

THE MERITS OF THE TRANSVAAL DISPUTE

IN contemporary disputes, passionate and partial assertion rarely fails to play as conspicuous a part as truth; with the result that there accumulates round the question at issue, and round the merits of the respective parties to it, a cloud of imperfect or erroneous statements, which not only confuse, but obscure. When such is the case, bystanders, who wish to understand, must be at the pains, first, to obtain a sufficient mastery of the various incidents and pleas which constitute the case on either side, and, second, to reject by elimination such of these attendant circumstances as are irrelevant or superfluous. The residuum of decisive factors, thus obtained, will commonly be found not too complicated or too doubtful to admit of a correct appreciation. The yield of the process will usually be twofold, viz., the facts, and the principle, upon both of which just judgment depends.

The dispute between Great Britain and the Transvaal, from which war has resulted, forms no exception to the general experience. On the contrary, passion and feeling, with their usual concomitant of hasty and vehement prejudgment, enter largely; while the facts of the case are numerous, and sufficiently complicated to require a very real mental effort to catalogue, comprehend, and appreciate them in their relative importance. I assume, however, that they are in their entirety sufficiently familiar to all readers of the "North American," through the numerous articles of the last three issues. It is fair, therefore, to presuppose some acquaintance with the detailed occurrences, extending over the past fifty or sixty years, which have resulted in the war of to-day. As a first elimination, it may be affirmed with probable exactness that the events and disputes precedent to the Pretoria Convention, in 1881, may now be dismissed from consideration. They possess, indeed, historical interest, useful to an understanding of conditions, but are no longer pertinent to the discussion of right. That Convention, with its successor, the London Convention of 1884, being acts in which both parties consented, regularized and legalized their political relations. Whatever the latter may previously have been, is now immaterial; the two conventions settled them then, and, conditional upon due observance on either side, remained the standard until the advent of war, which dissolves all conventions between belligerents, except such as pertain to the state of war itself. Our purpose here being to investigate the respective right and wrong, moral and political, in the conduct of both parties, which resulted in the quarrel, the outbreak of hostilities, in October, 1899, marks the termination, as the Convention of Pretoria, in 1881, marks the beginning, of the period under examination.

To make war is a moral action, to be judged by moral standards. The statement is applicable, not merely to the general question of waging war, but to all acts which lead up to war; as applicable to defensive war as to offensive. It is as wicked to maintain wrong by force as it is good to enforce right by arms, when it cannot be otherwise insured.

In political, as in personal, questions of moral conduct, I apprehend that judgment falls under three principal heads: Justice, Expediency or Policy, Duty. They answer to the questions:

Is this within my right? Is it wise to enforce it? Is it my duty to do so? As Saint Paul says, a thing may be lawful, but not expedient; the lawfulness and the expediency alike are elements of moral decision. Again, a man may without wrong waive a purely personal right, but when the rights of others are involved by the same concession, the question of duty to those affected enters; as, for instance, a father's action as affecting his children. The contemplated act may be lawful, it may be expedient at the moment, yet duty may forbid. By universal consent, Duty, when it clearly enters into a case, is paramount. It is the first in obligation, though not necessarily the first in order, of moral considerations.

War exists in South Africa because Great Britain has determinedly followed a certain course of action, which falls under two principal divisions: insistence, first, that a large alien population in the Transvaal must be relieved from grievous political and social wrongs under which it is laboring; and, second, that she has, in dealing with the Transvaal in this matter, a particular right and duty — as distinguished from those general rights which all nations possess as members of the international community. This particular right is called suzerainty, a term admittedly vague at the present day; that is, the word itself does not, in default of particular definitions, express the extent of the rights of the possessor — of the suzerain. It is inherited from the feudal system, where the obligations of tenure under a suzerain were of different kinds and degrees.

In the case of the Transvaal and Great Britain, the political relationship — independent of the word itself — is indicated by the character of the Conventions of Pretoria and of London. In both, the document is in the nature of a grant from a superior to a dependent.[1] The former and earlier consists of a " Preamble " and " Articles." The " preamble " expressly states, " On behalf of Her Majesty, that, . . . complete self-government, subject to the suzerainty of Her Majesty . . . will be accorded to the inhabitants of the Transvaal, upon the following terms and

[1] " When the Transvaal deputation visited the country in 1883, they asked, ' that the relation of a dependency, *publici juris*, in which our country now stands to the British Crown, may be replaced by that of two contracting Powers' (C. 3947, p. 5), and they submitted a draft treaty to give effect to their views. This draft treaty Lord Derby entirely rejected, observing that it was, 'neither in form nor in substance such as Her Majesty's Government could adopt.' " — Parliamentary Papers, C. 9507, p. 34.

conditions;" these terms, etc., being expressed in the "articles" — thirty-three in number. In the Convention of 1884, an introductory clause — not styled "preamble" in the document itself — reads: "Her Majesty has been pleased to take the said representations (of the Government of the Transvaal) into consideration, and has been pleased to direct, and it is hereby declared, that the following *articles* of a new Convention shall, when ratified by the Volksraad, be substituted for the *articles embodied* in the Convention of August 3, 1881."[1] In both cases there is a grant from one in authority over the other, the latter accepting; and in both cases terms — articles — are affixed to that grant of "complete self-government," which is the substance of each. It has been contended by the Transvaal statesmen that the omission, in the second convention, of the words, "subject to the suzerainty of Her Majesty," which were in the preamble of the first, abolished the suzerainty in fact. The sufficient reply to that is that the same construction abolishes the "complete self-government" granted; for the one phrase and the other occur only in the first Convention, in the preamble. To

[1] My italics.

the latter the second makes no allusion, but it is explicit as to the substitution of one set of articles for the other.

Sir Alfred Milner justly observed,[1] "Whether the relationship created by the Conventions is properly described as suzerainty is not, in my opinion, of much importance. It is a question of etymological rather than of political interest." Still, the tenacity with which the rulers of the Transvaal clung to the renunciation of the word has given it substantial significance; for, in the end, three months after Milner wrote the above sentences, they offered to concede nearly, if not quite, all that he had suggested for the benefit of the Uitlanders, upon two or three conditions, chief among which was that "a precedent shall not be formed by the present intervention for similar action in future," and "that Her Majesty's Government will not insist further upon the assertion of suzerainty, the controversy on this subject being tacitly allowed to drop."[2] This the British Government refused,[3] and the Transvaal withdrew its offer. It was too evident that the

[1] Parliamentary Papers, C. 9507, p. 6.
[2] Parliamentary Papers, C. 9521, p. 44.
[3] Ibid. pp. 45, 50; C. 9507, p. 33.

relinquishment of the word would be understood to mean a concession of non-dependence, and of non-responsibility to Great Britain, in all matters not expressly reserved. For the substance of suzerainty is the existence of dependence in the vassal, except so far as independence is conceded. "Complete self-government" is not independence. The explicit reservation by Great Britain of the right to nullify any treaty, or engagement, entered into by the Transvaal with a foreign country,[1] necessarily reserved with it responsibility for its relations with the outside world; for when treaties or engagements cannot be independently concluded, although dealings may be had and business carried on, it is impossible to guarantee satisfactory relations of any kind. The whole includes the parts; final ratification conditions and embraces all the antecedents.

The troubles which led up to this war sufficiently illustrate this. Among the Uitlanders in whose behalf Great Britain interposed were the subjects of many foreign States. In particular difficulties connected with these, the Transvaal agents might, by concession or otherwise, reach a satisfactory arrangement with the Powers con-

[1] Art. 4, Convention of 1884, Parliamentary Papers, C. 3914.

cerned, which might obviate the necessity of an engagement; but if it became necessary to enter into engagements, the reserved right of Great Britain entailed not only power, but responsibility, for the two are inseparable. Upon responsibility follows obligation — to procure a remedy for conditions provocative of just reclamation by foreign States; and this obligation outweighs, in moral force, that political expediency — or interest — which, by common consent, justifies interference in the affairs of a neighboring State, when these threaten your own peace or welfare, as, for instance, when we lately interfered with Spain in Cuba, a course in which our obligation was not legal, but moral. Our own keen national sense on this subject is evidenced by our Monroe Doctrine. In the Americas we object to foreign interference carried beyond certain limits, because the matter comes too near home for our peace and interest. Well, Great Britain, which rules by far the greater part of South Africa, and is predominant there as we are here, objects to foreign interference in the Transvaal, her statesmen having even used the Monroe Doctrine as illustrative of her policy in that respect. Consequently, when she established the Transvaal as a self-governing but dependent State, she, in addition to the right resting upon general interest in a neighbor, reserved a check upon its relations with foreign States.

The *right* to interpose as she has done — the first, in order, of the moral considerations — rests upon two grounds: First, of general policy, in the necessity of remedying conditions in a neighboring State, which threaten one's own tranquillity or welfare — as when we intervened in Cuba and in the Venezuela business; and, second, upon the specific right of suzerainty, retained in the Acts which constituted the Transvaal into the South African Republic. For those not satisfied, as I am, with the technical verbal argument in proof of this retention (given above), the purpose and understanding of the British Government in the transaction were affirmed in Parliament by its negotiator, Lord Derby, on March 17, 1884, the Convention, having been signed February 27, less than three weeks before. "It has been said that the object of the Convention had been to abolish the suzerainty of the British Crown. The word 'suzerainty' is a very vague word, and I do not think it is capable of any precise legal definition. Whatever we may understand by it, I think it is not very easy to define. But I apprehend, whether you call it a protectorate, of a suzerainty, or the recognition of England as a paramount Power, the fact is that a certain controlling power is retained when the State which exercises this suzerainty has a right to veto any negotiations into which the *dependent*[1] State may enter with foreign Powers. Whatever suzerainty meant in the Convention of Pretoria, the condition of things which it implies still remains; although the word is not actually employed, we have kept the substance. We have abstained from using the word, because it was not capable of legal definition, and because it seemed to be a word which was likely to lead to misconception and misunderstanding."[2] It is clear that Derby, overlooking the retention of the preamble of 1881, understood himself to have abandoned, not the thing, but the word, because the latter was indeterminate; owing to the historical applications which constitute its definition being so varied.

Passing with these remarks from the question of Great Britain's rights, I take up next that of her duty, under the conditions existing prior to

[1] My italic.   [2] Parl. Papers, C. 9507, p. 34.

the war; leaving to the end a brief summary of the reasons which, in my opinion, constitute the expediency, or policy, of her action in the premises.

It is a commonplace, that responsibility is the complement of power. It is also the foundation of duty. A person responsible has a duty to do, when occasion arises. In refusing the Transvaal that independence in foreign relations which would enable other States to hold it directly accountable, Great Britain retained, in so far, responsibility that foreigners should be so treated as to give no just ground for reclamations. In the case of wrongdoing by a dependent, one's duty, or responsibility, is not limited to correction upon complaint of grievance. Even for single, unforeseen, acts of wrong, reparation may be exacted; but for a continuous act, or condition, clearly known, the duty of remedial measures is such that the failure to institute them is just cause for complaint. A foreign State, in its care for its citizens abroad, does not, for redress, look below the supreme power of the State where they are domiciled. From the latter it demands justice, nor does it concern itself with the methods by which justice is reached; those are part of the internal affairs of the other country. The home government of the injured man sees only the injury and the responsible power; that is, the supreme Government. When Italian citizens were lynched in New Orleans some years ago, the Italian Government had before it two facts: violence done to its citizens, and the government of the country where the violence occurred. The laws and courts of the United States, State sovereignty, the laws of Louisiana, were nothing to it — part of the internal machinery of our Government. The injured persons and the responsible Power were the only things with which Italy then had concern.

The political relation of the Transvaal to Great Britain is certainly not the same as that of one of our States to the central Government; but Great Britain, by retaining the ultimate control of foreign relations, and by her well-defined purpose not to permit interference in the Transvaal by a foreign Power, was responsible for conditions of wrong to foreign citizens within its borders. She had surrendered the right to interfere, as suzerain, with internal affairs; but she had not relieved herself, as by a grant of full independence and sovereignty she might have done, from responsibility for injury due to internal mal-administration; any more than the United States was relieved of the responsibility to Italy by the State sovereignty of Louisiana. The responsibility thus remaining gave the right to require, not that this or that change should be made in the internal administration of the Transvaal, but that the condition of the foreign population should in some way be made socially and economically tolerable. The method was not her affair, but the result was. Internal affairs and external relations are logically separable; but mutual interaction takes place between them.

Citizens of other States, however, formed a minority of the Uitlander population; a majority were British subjects. To these the duty of Great Britain was that of a State to its citizens residing in foreign countries, everywhere throughout the world. If they received wrong, she had the duty of reclamation; if the wrong were continuous, she owed sustained diplomatic pressure for a change of action; if this were refused, she had, by international law, the right of war. When the exercise of this last right becomes a duty, is a question for the sole decision of the injured State. In this particular the Transvaal stood to her, by her own act, in the relation of an independent State. Control of internal affairs had been conceded to it, and to demand, as suzerain, a change of the laws, would have been to break the compact. "The British Government," says Mr. Bryce, "always admitted that they had no right to demand the franchise;"[1] an assertion which demonstrates the correctness of their attitude, and which is most fully substantiated by the papers submitted to Parliament. But it was no breach of compact to demand that existing wrongs should be righted, leaving to the Transvaal authorities the determination of the methods — the internal arrangements — by which the result was reached. Such pressure rests on international law, would be as applicable to a difficulty with the United States as to one with the Transvaal, and, if wrongs sufficiently great existed, it was the duty of Great Britain to exert such pressure. This was her second duty. There was a third that will be mentioned later.

Did such wrongs exist? In my judgment there certainly did, and of a character and extent that, if not remedied, would justify war. Of course, when one comes to estimate injury, great

[1] "Impressions of South Africa," Second Edition, p. xxxiv.

differences of opinion will be manifested. It is not every small wrong that makes it expedient to go to law; nor does even serious damage constitute an unendurable wrong. But, if it be hard to measure wrongs in degree, it is less difficult to value them in kind; to recognize an underlying principle, and to see that when this is violated by rulers, there is planted a root of bitterness which sooner or later must bear its evil fruit, and which therefore cannot be too soon extirpated. I prefer here, first, to state the character of the Transvaal Government in its relation to the Uitlanders in the words of Mr. Bryce, for not only are his moderation and candor universally recognized, but he has not approved the course of his own country in so far as war has by it been made inevitable. " The position of the Transvaal Government, although it had some measure of legal strength, was, if regarded from the point of view of actual facts, logically indefensible and materially dangerous. . . . They — or rather the President and his advisers — committed the fatal mistake of trying to maintain a government which was at the same time undemocratic and incompetent. . . . An exclusive government may be pardoned if it is efficient; an inefficient government, if it rests upon the people. But a government which is both inefficient and exclusive incurs a weight of odium under which it must ultimately sink; and this was the kind of government which the Transvaal attempted to maintain. They ought, therefore, to have either extended their franchise or reformed their administration."[1]

Reform of the franchise was what the British Government suggested, but could not demand; for it had no control of the internal affairs. But, underlying all this undemocratic and inefficient government, was unwillingness to acknowledge the fundamental principle, by the maintenance of which liberty has made each painful step upward, viz., that taxation rests in the hands of the taxed community, acting through its representatives, while enlargement of the basis of representation is one of the particular notes of modern political advance. The Uitlanders produced more than nine-tenths of the revenue, but the terms upon which they were admitted to the franchise were so exorbitant as to be prohibitory. Especially grievous was the condition that between naturalization and franchise a long period intervened, during which the man had lost his old citizenship

[1] "Impressions of South Africa," Second Edition, p. xviii.

without acquiring the privileges of the new. While in that position he was no man's man, having lost his hold on one country, while in the other he had obtained no right, but only duties; such as compulsory military service, and the payment of taxes, in the levying of which he not only had no vote at the polls, but no organ of speech, no adequate representative, in the deliberations of the Legislature.[1] The political sin of the Transvaal against the Uitlander, therefore, was no mere matter of detail — of less or more — but was fundamental in its denial of elementary political right.

Consider the conditions of the franchise in June last, at the time of the Bloemfontein Conference, between Sir Alfred Milner and President Krüger. In 1882, one year after the Convention of Pretoria, the period for attaining the full franchise, which in the earlier days of the community had been one or two years, was fixed at five years. In 1885 came the gold discoveries, with the inflow of the mining population, and in

---

[1] The gold fields, in which district live most of the Uitlanders, who alone are far more numerous than all the burghers in the Transvaal, had but two representatives in a House of 28. — C. 9404, p. 54.

1890 the time was extended to fourteen years. Nor was this all, although extremely oppressive, judged by all modern standards, when it is considered that the men to whom it applied were those who were developing the resources of the State and producing nine-tenths of its revenue. The law was made applicable to those already in the country; so that men who had entered in 1886 and the intervening years, however valuable as members of the community, were unable to acquire full citizenship in five years, according to the conditions of their immigration, but were compelled to wait fourteen. To this were attached other vexatious regulations, which made it an onerous task for a man to establish his claims, and left it in the power of the authorities to retard and thwart him in his effort to gain citizenship. Above all, by a singular provision then introduced, an interval of twelve years was interposed between naturalization and full franchise; the latter consisting in power to vote for members of the First Volksraad, in which the valid legislative power of the Republic is concentrated. During this period, a man, having become by naturalization a citizen of the Transvaal, lost the protection his native country would give him, in case of injustice, but acquired no real share in the government of his new State.

That any men of English or American origin would rest quietly under such political treatment is most improbable; but it is impossible unless administration be such as to give them all the benefits of pure and efficient government. This, however, was not the case, as Mr. Bryce has said. Into the details of mis-government there is not here space to go; they must be sought in the many books on the subject. A Boer partisan cynically observes, " In the Transvaal the poor have the power, and compel the rich to pay the taxes;"[1] the truth being, however, that an armed minority holds the power, compels the majority to pay the taxes, denies it representation, and misgoverns it with the money extorted.

Such internal administration must entail external complications. In the neighboring British colonies there is a large Dutch population, which everywhere possesses equal political rights with its British fellow-subjects. The wrath of the latter was stirred by the inequality and indignity suffered by their countrymen in the Transvaal; and the political agitation instituted by the Uit-

[1] Hillegas: "Oom Paul's People," p. 232.

landers was warmly seconded by the men of English blood in the surrounding districts. Both carried their appeals to the home Government, and the latter was made to feel that the loyalty and contentment of the colonist, upon which depends the integrity of the Empire, require that the latter not only be just itself, but shall exact justice for its citizens when clearly refused to them by others. That this view of the South African colonists was shared by the other parts of the Empire is shown by the enthusiasm with which, not Great Britain alone, but Canada and Australia espoused the cause of the Uitlander. The wrongs of the latter, by intensifying a common sentiment, have done more to rivet Imperial Federation than aught that planning and organization could contrive.

The British Government has for nearly a decade been confronted with the conditions which resulted last year in the Bloemfontein Conference. At this the British representative expressly disclaimed any intention of "giving orders or commands."[1] There had been long disagreements between the two States, which were increasing instead of diminishing. In his opinion,

[1] Parliamentary Papers, C. 9404, p. 16.

" the cause of the most serious differences arises out of the policy pursued by the Government of the South African Republic toward the Uitlander population." [1] If that " Government, of its own accord, would afford a more liberal treatment to the Uitlanders, this would not increase British interference, but enormously diminish it. If they were in a position to help themselves they would not always be appealing to us under the Convention." As a definite proposition he suggested that the full franchise should be given to every foreigner who had resided for five years in the Republic — thus reverting to the law of 1882. To this could be attached a property qualification which would prevent so many new voters as would outnumber the old burghers. Also, as the Uitlanders mostly live in one district of the Republic, and in order that their representatives should not be "in a contemptible minority," he proposed that there should be a certain number of new constituencies in the First Volksraad.[2]

The Conference separated without reaching an agreement. On June 15, the Raad adjourned, to allow members to consult their constituencies. On July 3 it reassembled, and in the course of

[1] Parliamentary Papers, C. 9404, pp. 14, 15.   [2] *Ibid.* p. 3.

the month passed an act granting naturalization and full franchise to residents of seven years, having certain property qualifications. Not only was the period thought too long, but to the process of obtaining these rights were attached conditions so complicated as to be unsatisfactory to the Uitlanders and to the British Government; for it was believed that they could, and would, be used to defeat the applicant. A request of the British Government for "an opportunity of making its views known on this new franchise law" was refused, on the ground that "the First Volksraad had now 'passed the law and finally fixed it.'"[1] Diplomacy cannot go on when one side invokes the law of its land to close discussion. The South African Republic overlooked the fact that, where parties disagree, agreement must mean acceptance by both, whether with or without war.

Being thus dissatisfied, the British Government, on August 1, invited the Transvaal to appoint delegates, to discuss with British delegates, whether "the Uitlanders will be given immediate and substantial representation by the Franchise Law recently passed, together with other measures connected with it — such as in-

[1] Parliamentary Papers, C. 9518, pp. 51, 58.

crease of seats — and, if not, what additions or alterations may be necessary to secure that result."[1] To this Commission of Inquiry the Transvaal Government was averse, assigning as its reason that joint inquiry would prejudice the right of full independence in internal affairs; and on August 15, intimated that it was "willing to make the following proposals, provided that Her Majesty's Government are willing not to press their demand for the proposed joint inquiry into the political representation of the Uitlanders."[2] These proposals were: A five years' retrospective franchise, which was Milner's suggestion at Bloemfontein; ten seats in a First Volksraad of thirty-six members; and certain other minor concessions.[3] With these propositions, however, were coupled three conditions, one of which was a provision for arbitration, to which the British Government acceded tentatively. The other two, already quoted, were: "That Her Majesty's Government will agree that the present intervention shall not form a precedent for future similar action, and that in the future no interference in the internal affairs of the Republic will take

[1] Parliamentary Papers, C. 9518, p. 30.
[2] Ibid. C. 9521, p. 44.   [3] Ibid. p. 46.

place; and that Her Majesty's Government will not further insist on the assertion of suzerainty."[1] The latter was refused; to the former the reply was that, "Her Majesty's Government cannot, of course, debar themselves from their rights under the Conventions, nor divest themselves of the ordinary obligations of a civilized Power to protect its subjects in a foreign country from injustice."[2] The British Government had not interfered in the internal affairs of the Transvaal, as implied by the latter. Seeing the oppression of its citizens there, and the resulting friction between the two governments, it had demanded relief, suggesting that a liberal franchise would most surely afford this, and it had refused to accept, as adequate, measures that in its judgment were inadequate; but further than suggestion no claim to intervention, as suzerain, was advanced. Of course, the compulsion of force — of possible war — hung in the background, as it does in all diplomatic disputes of a critical nature between States, even mutually independent.

Dissatisfied with this reply, the Transvaal withdrew its offer. The subsequent negotiations are important as elucidatory, but may be

[1] Parliamentary Papers, C. 9521, pp. 46, 47.   [2] Ibid. p. 50.

neglected, as not otherwise essential to the merits of the case. On October 9, the Transvaal issued its ultimatum. In my opinion, the question who declared war is immaterial, except for the moral effect upon the sentiment that condemns all wars, judges mainly by feeling and preconception, and looks little into causes. Briefly stated, the argument in my mind runs thus: There were in the Transvaal some sixty thousand Uitlanders and thirty thousand Boers[1] of an age fit for suffrage. Of the former the great majority were British subjects. They were oppressively misgoverned, and were denied both franchise and representation. In a Volksraad of twenty-eight there were from their district only two, in the choice of whom they had no adequate voice. They raised the revenue, from less than a million, to twenty million dollars. Their appeals for good administration and for fair treatment were disregarded. They had entered the country by encouragement of the Government,[2] many of them at a time when five years' residence conferred the franchise;

[1] President Krüger's estimate. — Parliamentary Papers, C. 9404, p. 19.
[2] Letter of Ewald Esselen, Secretary to Transvaal Deputation in London, December 21, 1883. *Contemporary Review*, February, 1898; Article, "Real Grievances of the Uitlanders."

but before they could obtain it the period was increased to fourteen years. The laws were unstable and easily altered; confused, purposely or not, so that the difficulties of qualifying were enormously increased. Unable to become citizens, unprotected, and unable politically to protect themselves, they appealed, as every domiciled foreigner does, to their home government. Innumerable complaints cumbered the files and embarrassed the relations of the two States. Agitation spread throughout South Africa, defining itself on lines of race feeling, never wholly extinguished, and threatening the deplorable antagonisms that thence arise. The elements of a conflagration were all there, and the atmosphere rising to the kindling point. To compose the trouble, Great Britain suggested a plan eminently reasonable, unfair only to the Uitlanders, to whom it gave far less than all white men throughout South Africa receive at British hands, and she refused to accept as satisfactory anything less than the minimum of remedy; for let it be continually remembered that the franchise was sought, not mainly as an act of justice, but as the most promising means of escape from a position become unendurable.

"The franchise," says Mr. Bryce, "did not constitute a legitimate cause of war."[1] In this it appears to me there is a confusion of idea, or a begging of the question. The question is begged, if it is implied that the cause of the war was a demand, based on suzerainty, for an extended franchise. That would not be a legitimate cause. But, in so far as a cause good in morals is legitimate, the denial of an adequate franchise was a legitimate cause of war, because, in the absence of an adequate alternative, it kept in a condition of intolerable oppression a number of British citizens who had been invited to commit their persons and their fortunes to the protection of the Transvaal Government, in order to develop the resources of the country. Great Britain had the highest moral duty to see that those people received — not the franchise necessarily — but fair treatment and decent government. There is not an American pro-Boer partisan that would have endured for six months the conditions of the Uitlanders, without appeal to his government, if it were in a position to aid.

That race differences were at the bottom of the war is an interesting philosophical explanation,

[1] "Impressions of South Africa," Second Edition, p. xxxiv.

and has its value. It is true, indeed, in great part, as a fact; for I trust no American or English community in the present day could, without its own blood boiling in its veins, give to any indwellers such treatment as the Boers have given the Uitlanders. But whatever part race differences have played, it has been as an ultimate cause, not as a proximate. The occasion of the war has been as described.

To the occasion, also, every consideration of duty and of expediency combined to compel Great Britain; to constitute a third duty already alluded to — the duty to the Empire. The peace of South Africa was not merely imperilled; it was destroyed, unless the conditions were healthfully and radically changed. Whether there was any widespread, organized conspiracy to supplant British rule by Dutch, is a matter only of inference; but it appears to me beyond doubt that a considerable number of Boers throughout South Africa cherished that purpose, consciously, and had succeeded in setting in motion feelings and conditions — of which the Transvaal was the centre — that would, unless abruptly checked, result in the subversion of British rule. We in America, who know the history of Secession, know to what lengths small beginnings, ably guided, can go. The political complexion, tenure, and stability of South Africa, however, are not a concern of the British Isles only, but of the British Empire. My professional opinion does not attach supreme, exclusive, naval importance to the Cape route as compared with that of Suez; but the mass of sound British opinion does, and its commercial value is beyond dispute. To India and to Australia it is of the first consequence; to Great Britain and to Atlantic Canada hardly less. The Cape is one of the vital centres in the network of communications of the whole Empire. To let it go, wrenched away through culpable remissness, would be to dissolve the Empire; and justly. A government is not worthy to live, that, having shown to all its subjects the impartiality and liberality which Great Britain has to British and Dutch alike throughout South Africa, should supinely acquiesce in the conditions of the Transvaal, as depicted, or fail to take heed that the Dutch Afrikander, as a class, has so little learned the lessons of political justice and true liberty, that his sympathies are with the Boer oppressor rather than with the Uitlander oppressed. Under such conditions it would have been imperial suicide to have allowed the well-known, though undervalued, military preparations of the Transvaal to pass unnoticed, defiant oppression to continue, and race disaffection to come to a head, until the favorable moment for revolt should be found in a day of imperial embarrassment. To every subject of the Empire the Government owed it to settle at once the question, and to establish its own paramountcy on bases that cannot be shaken lightly.

NOTE. — The Parliamentary Papers referred to in the footnotes contain the official correspondence of *both* parties to the negotiations.